Jay Unde

GHOST TRACKS

Surprising Stories of the Supernatural on Rails

**How death, disease, wrecks,
bridge curses and even ghosts
haunted Nova Scotia's railways**

Railfare ❋ DC Books

DEDICATION

"To my sister Sara,
who was part of my own 'ghost' story in 1971,
and my sister-in-law Kelly Steeves,
who always enjoys a good ghost tale."

Book designed and typeset in Adobe Garamond Pro, ITC Garamond, and Myriad MM by Eric Clegg with guidance from David Henderson.
Graphic grid designed by Primeau & Barey, Montreal.
Printed and bound in Canada by Transcontinental Printing.
Distributed by LitDistCo.

Legal Deposit, *Bibliothèque et Archives nationales du Québec* and the National Library of Canada, 2nd Trimester, 2009.

Library and Archives Canada Cataloguing in Publication
Underwood, Jay, 1958-,
Ghost tracks : surprising stories of the supernatural on rails / Jay Underwood.
Includes bibliographical references and index.
ISBN 978-1-897190-47-0 (pbk.)
ISBN 978-1-897190-48-7 (bound)
1. Ghost stories, Canadian (English).
2. Railroads--Canada--Folklore.
I. Title.
BF1472.C3U54 2009 133.1'22 C2009-900127-6

For our publishing activities, Railfare ❄ DC Books gratefully acknowledges the financial support of the governnment of Canada through the Book Publishing Industry Development Program (BPIDP).

 Canada Council for the Arts   Conseil des Arts du Canada

Société de développement des entreprises culturelles
Québec ✚✚

Railfare ❄ DC Books
Ontario office:
1880 Valley Farm Road, Unit #TP-27
Pickering, Ontario L1V 6B3

Business office and mailing address:
Box 666, St. Laurent Station,
Montreal, Quebec H4L 4V9
railfare@videotron.ca
www.railfare.net

About the Cover
A Canadian National Railways locomotive passes through the "hub town" of Truro, Nova Scotia, during the night, casting an eerie light in its path and wake. (Andrew Underwood)

CONTENTS

ACKNOWLEDGEMENTS

So much of this work was compiled with the help of tips from people who were reluctant to admit they believe in – much less had seen – ghosts, or who placed any credence in supernatural stories. Many others, however, were more than happy to assist with the assembling of factual details that could either support or refute the stories. On several occasions I imposed upon these good people more than once, and for their persistent patience I am doubly grateful.

Among them are Nan Harvey of the Colchester Historical Society in Truro, Nova Scotia, Rod Norrie, also of Truro, who started this project when he handed me a copy of the original story of the Merigomish wreck; Dr. Michael and Ethel Ojoleck of Judique; Leona Hussey of Sydney, who provided her manuscript of the Whiteside poltergeist, and Cape Breton genealogical researchers Allan J. Gillis, Maureen McNeill, and Anne Capstick. Again I must thank Ros Morrison, Karen King, and the staff of the Elmsdale branch Colchester-East Hants Regional Library, as well as the staff of Nova Scotia Archives & Records Management Service in Halifax, who were perhaps the most patient of all.

Many of my colleagues in the Nova Scotia Railway Heritage Society responded to my pleas for help, among them Bob Tennant of Halifax, the former editor of the Scotian Railroad Society newsletter *Maritime Express*; Art Clowes of Riverdale, New Brunswick who has always allowed me the use of his electronic scrapbook; Glen Smith of Port Morien, Cape Breton; and Herb MacDonald of Dartmouth.

Thanks also go out to Louise Higgs of the *Chronicle-Herald* library, Halifax, Bill Bussey of the Sydney & Louisburg Railway Museum, Barbara Spindler, office manager of the South Shore Genealogical Society, John Cotton, director of municipal recreation/tourism for Inverness County, Virginia MacIsaac of Judique, Ann Wallace of Monastery, Nova Scotia, Linda Darling, of the Antigonish Rootsweb list, Dr. Sally Rhine Feather of the Rhine Research Centre, University of North Carolina's Institute of Parapsychology, Frank Macdonald, publisher, and Rankin MacDonald, editor, of the *Inverness Oran* for helping spread the word about my interest in their local ghosts, and Brad Chisholm, compliance officer with the Nova Scotia Real Estate Commission.

My family – chiefly my son Andrew and brother Simon – again came to my aid, especially with the transportation to various sites, and photography of the eerie locations. Thanks too to my sister Sara for a timely tip. It was a sleepwalking Sara, who I thought I was assisting back to bed in Abingdon, England in 1971, when I had my first encounter with a ghost more than thirty-five years ago. Her daughter, Helen Livingston, assisted with the photography at Belmont. In that same vein I must thank my late maternal grandmother, Barbara (Murray) Joels, whose emphatic belief in the supernatural may have been the source of my fascination for this topic.

Help also came from April MacLean, Beaton Institute, University College of Cape Breton, in Sydney, Nova Scotia, and historians Alfreda Withrow, LeRoy Peach, and Barbara Peart, John Donald Cameron of the Judique Historical and Cultural Society,

Jan Blodgett, college archivist and records management coordinator at the E.H. Little Library of Davidson College, Donelda MacDonald of the Whitney Pier Historical Society, and Beryl MacDonald of the Gut of Canso Museum in Port Hawkesbury. Of invaluable assistance were the many participants on the Nova Scotia Rootsweb internet list who took time from their own genealogical research to answer my queries an offer new clues, especially in the search for the elusive Grey Lady of Judique.

Assisting me through the minefield of genealogy – where the names and dates from a variety of sources were frequently in conflict – were John Wilson of Alberton, Prince Edward Island, Ardella MacPhee of New Glasgow, Patricia Lumsden of the Guysbrough County Genweb list, and Marie P. Connolly of the Nova Scotia Rootsweb list. Linda Burtch of the Public Library of Sault Ste. Marie (Ontario) Archives came through with the Clergue photograph. Also worthy of special mention is Diana Lyn Tibert of Milford Nova Scotia, a researcher of Guysborough County genealogy, and newspaper columnist. Her column *Roots to the Past* appears in many Atlantic Canadian newspapers.

Finally thanks go again to my publishers for recognizing that railway folklore is as important a part of railway history as the names and dates of the promoters and their plans, the surveyors and their schemes, and the myriad technical details of steam and diesel locomotives. Too often these cultural aspects of railways are overlooked by historians, or dismissed by others as insignificant flights of fancy.

Jay Underwood
Elmsdale, Nova Scotia
January 2009

INTRODUCTION

T HIS project was undertaken with some reservation, not the least of which was a concern about how it would be received by followers of "serious" railway history. It would have been folly to risk opprobrium for the sake of an anthology of stories that could be subjected to accusations of invention and imagination. (In the interest of full disclosure, I cannot claim to be without bias when I write of such things as ghosts; I feel I saw one, as a youngster in England, and the experience was real and frightening.) But as an adult, a trained journalist, and a student of railway history, I approached these stories intent upon using facts to prove or discredit the lore, or at least to provide some context and explanation as to how it was that they have been proliferated.

In this way, I hope to avoid the criticism that has been meted out to journalist Bill Jessome for his efforts in three books, two of which – *Maritime Mysteries (and the ghosts that haunt us)* (Nimbus, 1999) and *More Maritime Mysteries* (Nimbus 2001) – were critiqued by Tom Knapp, of the on-line regional cultural arts magazine Rambles (January 2002). Knapp noted:

"The author seems to exhibit a lack of curiosity about many of these tales. He relates some ghost stories without delving very deeply into the background of the haunted location or the possible identity of the spirit in question. It seems he often just passes on stories exactly as told to him, without bothering to do even simple research."

In that sense, Jessome was simply carrying on a tradition practiced by a former colleague of his – and mine – the late Roland Sherwood, the veteran journalist from Pictou County, whose books on Maritime region lore were simply stories passed on, and retold in a familiar way. It is worth noting that Rollie Sherwood's largest anthology of such stories, *Maritime Mysteries: Haunting Tales from Atlantic Canada* – (Lancelot Press, Hantsport Nova Scotia, 1976), has no railway content in any of the nineteen tales he recounts.

In fairness, Sherwood and Jessome were faced with the problem that such events rarely came with substantial evidence to prove or disprove their veracity. In this regard I am fortunate. The railway is the only industry that has been watched since its inception by a news media often determined to expose the weak underbelly of the political or capitalist masters, searching for any sign of vulnerability that would advance an editorial stand. That is why newspaper accounts form such a great part of the evidence presented here, so intent was the coverage until the post-Second World War era that even such details as supernatural episodes were not allowed to go unrecorded.

Certainly invention would have been an easy matter. The story of the Whiteside poltergeist presented such an opportunity, because with the date of the incident so uncertain, other events could have been woven into the fabric of the story to create an entirely credible tale. Take the death of Laurie MacIntosh, for example. During the course of my investigation into the Whiteside haunting, I was approached – coincidentally – by the grandson of this Canadian National Railways engineer who died in a wreck at Heatherton on April 17th 1935. Chris Moreau was seeking more detail about the incident and proposing that his grandfather be highlighted on the website of the Nova Scotia Railway Heritage Society. MacIntosh had returned to the railway in 1919 after serving in war-torn Europe, and like many other young Canadians who went to serve king and country, had brought back a pretty war bride. Moreau told me that his grandfather was killed when his train derailed, but his actions – and those of his fireman, the other victim of the wreck – saved lives. The only compensation offered to McIntosh's widow was a lifetime pass on the railway. As the result of this niggardly charity, Moreau's mother and his uncle were raised suffering the depredations that so often accompanied such misfortune. Heatherton is only a matter of miles from Havre Boucher, the apparent scene of the wreck that gave rise to the Whiteside poltergeist, and it would have been convenient to fabricate the fiction that the phantom was the spirit of MacIntosh, a "wrath version" of the phenomenon, one who had returned to vent his rage over the treatment his family had received from a government to which he had given so much.

There are two incidents in this collection that are undoubtedly false. The Halifax bridge curse is certainly the fiction of a Halifax newspaper that has since passed into other hands, so it is unreasonable to hold the current owners accountable. The perpetrators have long since passed on to their own rewards. The Upper Tantallon ghost is likewise a fable – to a certain point – because the railway records do not support the story of the drunken station agent being struck by a train. Neither do the newspaper records, any one of which would have played the story well, in order to hold the government accountable for some real or imagined evil. The noises heard in the station are probably real and no doubt alarming. The possibility that a ghost exists within that building cannot be discounted, and this work is not intended to refute the former owner's claims. The railway roots of the story, however, are questionable.

That these stories are part of legitimate railway history cannot be disputed. It is as lore, however, that these stories have their value, for they are the intangible and very human side of an industry that is governed by science, technology and the unrelenting regulation of the timetable and operating rule book. Indeed, it may be that for many employees who followed all those rules and regulations to the best of their ability, the supernatural could be the only explanation when something went terribly wrong and the life of a co-worker or member of the public was lost.

Despite their antiquity, the stories featured here do not serve as nostalgic reminders of how people once regarded the "new" technology of the railway, which encroached upon every aspect of the "old ways." Superstitions still abound. How else can one explain why some people lift their feet when they drive over railway tracks, and simultaneously make a wish for good luck? What of the superstition of the necessity of women lifting up their feet and touching a screw while they cross the tracks, so they won't get pregnant? Similarly how does one explain the superstition of touching glass when going over railroad tracks… for good luck?

As to the validity of these tales, it is for readers to judge for themselves. What this work attempts to do is add to the reader's general knowledge of Nova Scotia's railway history. Perhaps – when all is considered – the fact that so many of these tales have their roots in the late 19th Century, means they represent nothing more than a reaction to what Ralph Allen (*Ordeal by Fire*, Doubleday, 1961) called "a wondrous new age," as Canadians recovered from the national trauma of the Boer War and the death of a queen:

"A new current was in motion within the mainstream of human history. The railways opened up a new caravan trail for the restless, the driven, and the questing and led them to the heartland of Canada. The travellers set forth on many impulses and from many places: some drawn by fear, some by ambition, some by faith, some by gullibility."

Jay Underwood
Elmsdale, Nova Scotia
January 2009

ABOUT THE AUTHOR

Jay Underwood is a graduate of the journalism program of Holland College of Applied Arts and Technology in Charlottetown, Prince Edward Island. Jay began his career in newspapers as a nightshift proof reader and obituary writer with the Charlottetown *Guardian-Patriot*. He then moved to the New Glasgow, Nova Scotia *Evening News*, as a reporter-photographer, and to the Truro, Nova Scotia *Daily News* as city editor. Briefly serving as city editor at the Timmins, Ontario *Daily Press*, he returned to Nova Scotia as editor and publisher of the Springhill-Parrsboro *Record*, and the Enfield *Weekly Press*, before joining the staff of the Halifax *Daily News* as senior copy editor and a member of the editorial board.

Disabled by complications of diabetes that took most of his sight in 1999, Jay focused on his love of history and railways, producing *Ketchum's Folly* in 1995, and *Full Steam Ahead: The life and locomotives of Alexander Mitchell* in 1996 (Lancelot Press), and, more recently, *Built for War: Canada's Intercolonial Railway* (Railfare*DC Books) in 2005, and *From Folly to Fortune* (Railfare*DC Books) in 2007.

Now in his fifth term as president of the Nova Scotia Railway Heritage Society, Jay and his colleagues were successful in preventing the historic 1905 vice-regal railway car *Alexandra* from being scrapped, and the car is now being relocated to a museum site at Tatamagouche, Nova Scotia for restoration and public display. The society is planning to establish a permanent archive and library offering educational and genealogical information to Nova Scotians.

He is a frequent contributor to *Canadian Rail*, the journal of the Canadian Railroad Historical Association, and has plans for other books in the near future. His work centres on topics not previously covered by conventional history texts. Jay lives in Elmsdale, Nova Scotia with his wife Kathy and sons Derek and Andrew, who are employed as railway freight conductors with Canadian National Railway in Halifax, Nova Scotia.

CHAPTER 1

The Hoodoo Locomotive and the Cobequid Road Ghost

Part One: Samuel Trider's Last Ride

"Many an old head in the railroad game has had experiences he can't explain on a rational basis. His subconscious mind dwells in a spirit land of hoodoos and guardian angels, dreams and phantoms, hunches and unlucky numbers. He believes that in some inexplicable manner he receives advance warnings of impending disaster. As a rule these presentiments are too vague for practical use but on numerous occasions they have led to the saving of human life."

- Freeman Hubbard, *Railroad Man's Magazine*, April 1949

IN his book about Nova Scotia ghosts Darryl Walsh makes note of a ghastly apparition at Windsor Junction. His story tells of two children playing at the grade crossing on Cobequid Road, who notice a strange woman walking by the tracks. Their attention is then caught up in the passing of a train – the road crosses Canadian National Railways' main line out of Halifax – and when they look back towards the woman, she has vanished:

"By the children's description of the woman, the parents were able to determine she was someone who had died a few years previously. Her husband worked for the railway company at the time. The next day he was killed by a train at the same spot where the children had seen his ghostly wife twenty-four hours before."[1]

The lack of specific detail – names and dates in particular – could lead to the conclusion that the event involving children belongs in the realm of "urban mythology," but there is a bigger story to this brief tale, involving a locomotive once thought to be haunted by its own ghosts and "hoodoos."

In the world of steam locomotive engineering, there is a colourful lexicon of names applied to various types of engines: Moguls, Pacifics, Decapods, Mikados. Built by Dickson of Scranton, Pennsylvania, the ill-fated 4-6-0 locomotive No. 1250, was originally shipped as Intercolonial Railway No. 63 on April 4 1902 3. (The 4-6-0 indicates the engine had four wheels on the leading truck – often called the pilot, or pony truck – and six driving wheels, with no trailing wheels.) The 4-6-0 type was burdened with the inelegant name of "Ten Wheeler."

On arrival at Moncton, New Brunswick, the engine was re-numbered IRC 239 to avoid confusion with a still-active Manchester-built 4-4-0. (IRC was used to designate the Intercolonial, and avoid confusion with the ICRR, Illinois Central Railroad). In the following year, after building 1,400 locomotives of its own since 1862, Dickson joined the four other manufacturers that became American Locomotive Co. (ALCO) to better compete against Baldwin's virtual monopoly on the market.

The numbering is significant. As Freeman Hubbard, long-time railroad storyteller for a popular American magazine has noted, superstitions often start with an incident that might have no credibility with what he called "analytical minds: "Repetitions of such incidents may breed a fear that becomes chronic. A locomotive involved in one or more wrecks is supposed to be jinxed, especially if she has a 13 or a 9 in her number. Enginemen fight shy of her."[2]

The superstitious might note that the 6 and 3 of Intercolonial Railway No. 63 add up to nine, and the second number assigned by the Intercolonial, IRC 239, had a 9 in it. It would seem the portents for misfortune were in place long before the engine saw service. Once on the job, the locomotive quickly ran into troubles, meeting with its first wreck after just eight months in service. The newspaper coverage of these events was quite thorough, although not entirely accurate, as will be seen later, and might today seem somewhat sensationalized.

Train wrecks were irresistible to newspapers. Such calamities had never been so accessible to reporters. The downtown fire might occasionally liven up a slow news day, but they were rare occurrences compared with a train derailment. Marine disasters provided stories involving great loss of life and heroics, but they too were scarcities, and when they occurred it was usually miles out at sea, and could only be reported days after the news had already been spread by telegraph, or as survivors were brought ashore by rescue ships. Unfortunately a wreck on the Intercolonial was a common occurrence, even if the term was frequently stretched to include everything from a simple derailment to a runaway boxcar, or a head-on collision between trains. In presenting the opportunity for dramatic hyperbole, the train wreck just couldn't be matched.

As it was, many newspapers developed a certain expertise in reporting railway accidents, and as the reports of the wrecks involving engine No. 239 will show, the major dailies in the region lost no time in disseminating complete, often lurid accounts, fresh from the scene. One authoritative journal of record was Moncton's *Daily Transcript*, which had a pro-employee stance. The coverage of No. 239's Belmont, Nova Scotia, wreck of December 6th 1902 was the first in a litany of graphic accounts of how Train No. 25, run by the Intercolonial as a Canadian Pacific Express from Halifax to Saint John New Brunswick, then to Montreal, took the lives of veteran engineer Samuel Trider, fireman Harry Campbell and four passengers, and left seven other passengers seriously injured.[3] It may have escaped the notice of the media at the time, perhaps it was simply an uncanny coincidence, but the number of casualties and fatalities amounted to thirteen people.

The Moncton *Daily Transcript* of December 8th provided part of what was to become a graphic litany of the events and aftermath of the wreck, noting the youthful toll included William Kennedy, age 23, of Black Rock, Newfoundland; 45-year-old W.B. McDonald, of Cambridge, Massachusetts; Malcolm McLean, 27, of Alberton, Prince Edward Island; 25-year-old Philip Toole; William Wall, age 25, of Hoche Cove, Newfoundland, and 28-year-old Minnie F. Croke, of Halifax, was returning to Waverley, Massachusetts, where she was employed.

Sam Trider was a legend in his time, a veteran of the railway who took the first Intercolonial train from Truro to Moncton when the line was opened in 1872. During

Left: VIA Rail's west-bound *Ocean* passes the cemetery at Belmont, Nova Scotia, where engineer Sam Trider took his last ride. (Jay Underwood)

his career he had been involved in a number of incidents, the most notable of which, to that time, had been the wreck at Palmer's Pond near Sackville, New Brunswick in 1897, which had resulted in the death of two passengers, and serious injury to a federal cabinet minister. It should be noted, however, that no significance was attached to the frequency of Trider's accidents. In fairness, the Palmer's Pond wreck was ruled not to be Trider's fault. That wreck has made its way into local lore because of the bounty bestowed upon residents of the area, who rushed to the scene to find the embankment literally knee-deep in newly minted bronze pennies.

Behind schedule after leaving Halifax, Trider was trying to make up time on a sharp bend in the track beyond Sackville, and the load of 5.6 tons of coins (80 boxes) shifted, throwing the cars down the embankment. The subsequent investigation showed all the boxes had been improperly piled at one end of the car.

Another incident had Trider at the mercy of the weather, but he acted heroically in avoiding any loss of life:

"Several years ago as Mr. Trider was holding the throttle pushing over the Tantramar marsh, he saw the tide which had burst through the dykes rolling up ahead of them to the road bed. He pulled the engine open but ran into the washout. The engine was completely under water which had risen with wonderful rapidity. The cab had been torn off and after the train had come to a standstill and the thoroughly shaken passengers had got themselves together, they were surprised to find driver Trider with his head above the water and holding his fireman, who was of small stature, with his head above the water. The driver and fireman were soon extricated from their unpleasant position none the worse except for a severe soaking."[4]

Trider's record, while acknowledged, does not appear to have been considered as a contributing cause of the Belmont wreck, despite a report that indicated he was also speeding along at Belmont, in an attempt to make up lost time. In its report of December 8th, the *Transcript* presented further graphic accounts, and a complete accounting of the dead that left the ominous number thirteen out of the equation, but left nothing to be said for the lucky number seven.[7] Perhaps one of the survivors may have credited his good fortune to divine intervention. Reverend and Mrs. Allan M. Hill, of Fairville, where Hill was pastor of the Presbyterian church, were passengers in the first class day coach. They had been spending a vacation in Halifax and were returning home to Saint John. He described a scene of complete terror that the newspaper interpreted as "tragic and thrilling details." In Hill's account, the speed of the train becomes a factor in the wreck, far more likely than any as yet unmentioned "hoodoo," when he suggests the train was "trying, I learned, to make up lost time.[8] This same accusation had been leveled at Trider in connection with the Palmer Pond wreck.

At this point the newspaper's report went into salacious detail that would only add to the macabre fascination people would develop for such accidents, making false the claims of many that today's mass media has invented the sensational reporting so often encountered and condemned. Significant in the account was the name of a passenger from Newfoundland, identified later as William Wall, who had been "horribly bruised by flying wood, but was conscious and trying, to all within his power, to aid those suffering around him."[9] Wall would quickly die from the wounds he received in the wreck.

Even those most cynical of superstition are aware that many people believe bad luck comes in "threes." For the family of Sam Trider, it came in spades, and yet no newspaper made the connection. Belmont was his third significant wreck.

Samuel M. Trider was listed in the 1901 census (Westmoreland, New Brunswick) as having been born July 7th 1848. He was married to Marguerett F. Trider, and their four sons were: Sylvester M., born September 25th 1882; Elmo M., born March 12th 1888; Wilfred S. M., born July 11th 1890; and Roy A.V.M., born March 2nd 1895. (It would be easy to believe that the "Tri-" in the family name alluded to the number three, but it is the English form of the German name, Treuter.) Samuel Trider is buried in Truro's Robie Street cemetery. [10]

Marguerett Slack was Samuel Trider's second wife. His first marriage appears to have been unlucky. His wife Sarah Slack died in February of 1877, just four months after giving birth to their daughter Sarah. Little Sarah died in August of 1877, at ten months of age. Three of Trider's children by his second marriage are interred with him at Truro: Eugene W. died May 6th 1889, aged four years; Vernon died August 2nd 1892, aged six weeks, and Vera Q.H., who died August 23rd 1897, aged six months. [11] Trider came from Three Miles Plains, Nova Scotia, and every railway man must have noticed the significance of the number of the train – the No. 9 train to Moncton – that took his body home.[12]

Not content to accept that the Belmont wreck was an accident, the newspapers rapidly sought the cause of the calamity, and were just as quick to find culprits not related to any hexes, curses, or hoodoos. In its December 16th edition, the Halifax *Herald*'s Truro correspondent noted that the pilot of the locomotive (the part of the train commonly called the "cowcatcher") had been damaged in a slight collision in the yard at Truro. The pilot, it was alleged, became loose, and was eventually torn off when it struck the bridge at Belmont. This cause was deemed "possible and quite probable" by the newspaper, although it was admitted the snowdrifts in the area at the time could have been a factor.[13]

Above: The scene of the wreck near Windsor Junction,
restored from the original print in the Halifax *Chronicle*.
(Jay Underwood collection)

The Moncton *Transcript* was quick to press its anti-government case in the December 17th edition, blaming insufficient facilities at Truro for the lack of repairs to the damaged locomotive, and Charles Tupper took the brunt of the blame. An unnamed "railway man" claimed he had sent a petition to the Conservative government in 1887 about the unsafe conditions at the Truro roundhouse, and had been rebuffed with statements that the facilities were sufficient. Tupper, it was claimed, made a similar statement in 1896: "He was approached during the time he was Minister of Railways and Canals, but discouraged the men of Truro, who asked for the Intercolonial Railway roundhouse to be rebuilt or repaired"[14]

There were many accidents on the Intercolonial in the period in which the Belmont wreck occurred. The railway was experiencing rapid growth, especially on its line to Cape Breton, where new mills had begun shipping steel to Montreal and Hamilton on track that was inadequate for such heavy traffic. With political pressure being brought on the government to reduce spending on the Intercolonial, many track improvements were left in abeyance, with the train crews paying the price. It wasn't until 1904 that the government announced a major renovation of sections of the line prone to accidents, or in dire need of repair. The question that was neither asked nor answered, however, is why driver Trider – or anyone else – did not inspect his locomotive for damage after the collision in the Truro yard? Surely a dislodged pilot would have been visible and should have been repaired before the train took its passengers out? The answer may lie in the adoption of assigned crews, which did not take place until the following decade.

Part Two: A Wreck at the Junction

Engine 239's second accident elicited no particular excitement in the press at the time. The incident was briefly referred to in the Moncton, New Brunswick, *Daily Times* edition of April 12th 1903, when it reported the train had run off the track at Humphrey's Mills, 3.2 kilometers (two miles) from Moncton while working "a train of immigrants."[15]

Immigrant trains were frequent on the Intercolonial, transporting the new arrivals from the port at Halifax westward to the prairies, where the Dominion government had concentrated its settlement schemes. Typically these trains would carry as many as two hundred passengers in what were called "colonist" cars, former passenger coaches that were considered too dilapidated for regular passenger use, and converted into sleeping cars that offered spartan accommodation.

Both the Intercolonial and Canadian Pacific offered this form of transportation to immigrants who purchased their tickets from Canadian agents in their homelands. The ticket covered the train and steamer transportation. When a CPR train travelled over Intercolonial tracks, (the CPR line ran from Saint John to Montreal, Quebec, through northern Maine and the Quebec Eastern Townships), however, it required an Intercolonial engine at its head to act as a "pilot," the Intercolonial engineer being more familiar with the regulations as well as the peculiarities and character of the road.

The lack of any fatalities at the Humphrey's derailment made this event one of the everyday occurrences in the operations of the Intercolonial, where delays were frequently experienced from track blocked by derailments, run-away cars, snowdrifts, stray cattle, or obstacles placed there by miscreants both mischievous and malicious.

A typical example of these perils can be found in driver William Wall's narrow escape from death or serious injury in November of 1902, just five months before his demise near the same spot. This was not the William Wall who had died at the Belmont wreck scene after trying to save lives, but the coincidence is eerie. The Moncton *Daily Transcript* of November 3rd 1902 reported that two boys had opened the switch at Lakeview, nineteen kilometers (twelve miles) from Halifax:

> "…where it could not be seen more than 200 yards ahead, and when the Sydney flyer of the I.C.R. came along at 35 miles an hour it dashed into a blind siding. Driver Wall was on the engine, and when he saw what was ahead he shut off steam, applied the air brakes, and jumped. A coal car was standing on the siding. The train ran into this and pushed it along till the small station beyond was reached. This building was forced ahead the length of the locomotive, which sank in the soft earth beneath. The passengers were badly shaken up but none was seriously hurt. Driver Wall sustained no injury, but his fireman William Purcell, had his shoulder dislocated." [16]

Such pranks were commonplace, especially around Hallowe'en – most were discovered long before the train reached the obstacle – and they were anticipated even by the most superstitious of railroaders, but it was engine No. 239's third wreck, just weeks after the run-off at Humphrey's Mill, that may have begun to unsettle the nerves of Intercolonial men, for as Hubbard has noted, the third time was considered "a charm." The Halifax *Morning Herald* of Monday April 13th 1903 offered generous detail in its coverage of the April 11th accident, quickly picked up by other regional newspapers.

Above: The locomotives at the wreck near Windsor Junction, in which William Wall died in 1903. (Robert W. Tennant Jr. collection)

In doing so, the Halifax paper may also have exposed the origin of Walsh's Cobequid Road ghost.

Travelling at forty miles an hour, Wall was at the throttle of Train No. 26, the Halifax-bound express from Montreal, when it ran headlong into the Sydney (Cape Breton) freight, traveling from Halifax at twenty miles an hour, four kilometers (two and half miles) north of Windsor Junction. According to the *Herald*, "the cause of the awful catastrophe, involving four lives and much valuable property, was the culpable neglect of the driver of the Sydney freight – Nelson Copeland."[17]

From the outset Nelson Copeland was saddled with the burden of the blame for the wreck, but the story was not without what the newspaper called its own "mystery."

Quoting fully from the train orders of the day, proof was given that Copeland had been ordered to stop at Windsor Junction to wait while the late incoming express driven by William Wall passed through:

"But driver Copeland did not slack up nor stop at Windsor Junction. He sped on as though he were in charge of an express train and had the right of way over the road, heeding not the fact, which he must have known, that the Montreal express was not far ahead on the way to meet him."[18]

Copeland wasn't the only man on the Sydney freight who knew that the train should have waited at the junction. According to the *Herald* "any man who had eyes could see for himself the red lights hard against any advance and the moonlight was almost clear enough to show the semaphore stretching out toward the track."[19] The rules of the road at the time were clear on this point. Before a train could leave a station, the driver and the conductor were furnished with an order showing their run and where the next approaching train was to be crossed. The station agent copied the order in triplicate, and before the train could leave, a copy was retained by the stationmaster and had to be signed by the conductor as an assurance that he had seen the orders. According to the *Herald* "this was done and all hands on the freight knew that the cross was to be made at the Junction."[20]

The *Herald's* coverage of this wreck shows the depth of the newspaper's resources, and the details they could muster independently of the scene of the accident. Certainly the major newspapers had reporters or correspondents who were keenly attuned to the gossip of the railway workplace, and yet while they were not loath to report rumour (such as the drinking habits of certain employees), they refrained from alluding to the superstitious.

In its reporting on the Windsor Junction wreck, the *Herald* showed it had staff members who had intimate knowledge of how a freight train was controlled, and understood that the engineer was under the orders of his conductor, and received information from his brakeman when things such as missed traffic orders were encountered.

Still, the newspaper was unwilling to believe that Copeland alone bore the responsibility, and worried openly that "if he dies before being able to speak, his secret will die with him." The general impression was that "absolute carelessness" caused the wreck, but the *Herald* wondered aloud, what about Copeland's conductor and brakeman? It was agreed that it was hard to imagine "that all three men should make a similar mistake in their orders, for what one knew, all knew."

The wreck took Michael Oakley, Wall's fireman; Edward Hill, Copeland's fireman; and Alfred Thorpe, Copeland's brakeman to their deaths. The newspaper also dismissed the rumour that the engineer had gone insane, noting that Hill and Thorpe should have been able to overpower him. The most reasonable theory, the reporter pondered aloud, was that Copeland's train became "unmanageable," and that he was unable to stop it.

The story was not without its heroes. Brakeman MacDonald was lauded for his devotion to duty when he jumped from Copeland's speeding train to signal in order to warn the staff at Windsor Junction, and Conductor Haynes received similar praise for his daring as he ran across the tops of the boxcars between his caboose and the locomotive in an attempt to warn Copeland. This brave act only elicited another question from the diligent reporter: " Why did not the conductor signal with his bell rope to the driver when he saw the mistake that had been made?"[21] Providing his own answer, the reporter noted no signal could be passed over a train of 87 cars such as the Sydney freight, by a bell rope. The rope might have worked effectively only on a train of half that length, and the only time a signal could be heard on a long freight train was when cars broke away.

The description of the location of the wreck, and the photographs of the accident, more accurately places it at what is known today as Nelson's Pond, closer to the community of Kinsac than Windsor Junction. At the end of a curve, two and a half miles beyond Windsor Junction, and four miles south of Wellington station, there is water on both sides of the track, which is an embankment ten or fifteen feet high. This location made rescue efforts difficult.

Above: Intercolonial Railway wrecking cranes gather the baggage car from Nelson's Pond, at the site of the 1903 wreck of Locomotive No. 239.
(Robert W. Tennant Jr. collection)

William Wall received posthumous heroes' honours as his express came through a cutting, around a curve, and onto a straightaway of about 1,000 yards of clear track between the two engines:

"His hand sprang to the throttle lever, he shut off steam and he applied the brakes. Never for a moment did he flinch from his post of duty, nor did his fireman move. They stuck to their engine like men. It was only for a moment, though, that the ordeal lasted, for the two trains very quickly covered the brief space between them. The engines crashed together with fearful impact, the sound of the collision being heard as far way as Bedford. While the railway men at the Junction knew of the impending disaster, two miles beyond, the great engines were in an embrace of death and four men were in the agonies of death. The engine of the freight and that of the express telescoped one another, and the freight cars piled up in a mass of indescribable confusion."[22]

While references to railway superstition were absent from the report, the *Herald* was not above employing dramatic hyperbole to increase the emotional appeal of the story. This included alluding to the image of the locomotive engineer as a "knight of the footplate," a romantic image still pervasive in the 1920s as J.F. Gairns indicates in *Railways for All.* Gairns called the express driver "a most enviable individual," who had risen through "most of the drudgery of his profession" to a position that offered both responsibility and the exhilaration of traveling as fast as eighty-five miles per hour "whirling past roadside stations with barely a warning whistle, and carrying behind him, perhaps the elite of the land, "all sorts and conditions of men" from the King downwards."[23]

This romantic notion is tempered somewhat by the reality of the locomotive crew's job, as described by the Brotherhood of Locomotive Engineers in its on-line history of the union:

"Railroading over a hundred years ago was a hazardous and dirty occupation. Soft coal smoke and black soot liberally covered the countryside, the train, and the engine. Those in the engine cab were coated with grime after every trip. Although the discomforts were many (hot in summer, cold and drafty in winter), the locomotive engineer had greater trials to face than this. He worked for a low rate of pay and he was often kept on the road for long periods of time, needing rest and fighting sleep. Yet he was put in charge of trainloads of goods or passengers and expected to be alert at all times, being paid on the basis of the run he made rather than the time spent on duty."[24]

It was conditions such as these, along with mechanical failures on the engines, that led to the high rate of wrecks, the union claims. The engineer also had some less-than-heroic chores to perform in the course of his employment. While supposedly at "rest" between assignments and often far from home, he was expected to overhaul pistons, valve stems, pumps, and clean headlights, "filling lamps, lubricating moving parts, or otherwise generally engaged in repairs on his engine."[25]

The death toll at Windsor Junction was limited, fortunately, by the small number of passengers on the train (trains so close to Easter were usually crowded) and the presence of two doctors on board the express, both of whom went to the aid of Copeland and those not evidently dead, like the tramp, Angus Macready, whose miraculous escape only added to the fable. Macready had been allowed by Wall (against standing orders of the railway) to ride on the engine from Truro to Halifax. A printer on his way to find work in Halifax, he was believed to have been "beating his way" from Pictou County and was put off the first train, only to get kinder consideration from Wall when his express stopped at the station. He offered a full eyewitness description of his experience to the *Herald* reporter:

"I saw nothing but suddenly I felt as if she had bursted. There seemed to be a terrible crack as if everything were getting to bits and I felt a 'lift' and then found myself fighting hot scalding steam. My first sensation was that of sinking and sinking, as if I was going through to the railway ties. Then came an enormous 'lift,' wrenching me awfully and throwing me in the air. I knew nothing more till I came to and found myself lying on the bank a few yards from the wrecked engine. During the very few moments that I was conscious and while these terrible things were happening, I saw and knew nothing of my companions in the engine cab. I did not know either Wall or Oakley, who allowed me on the engine solely out of kindness to an unknown and poor man who asked them for a favor. When I found myself on the bank I tried to rise, but it was impossible for me to do more than raise myself on my hands and knees. My back felt as if it were broken."[26]

Contained in the body of the lengthy newspaper account was a significant detail about Sydney freight engineer Nelson Copeland's physical state that could have condemned him. The *Herald* reporter noted that Copeland had arrived at Richmond yard in the dark and navigated his engine competently through the terminal to his waiting train of 87 cars without incident. He had then driven as far as Windsor Junction, which included the track up the ruling grade at Bedford station, without demonstrating any symptoms of drowsiness or mental incapacity.

The newspaper account of the condition of the locomotives leaves only wonderment that engine No. 239 was ever brought back into service, but a connection was made between the earlier wreck at Belmont, and a train that had carried the other William Wall to his maker:

"One of the locomotives, 239, that caused the disaster at Belmont and which Samuel Trider piloted to his death was again a leading actor in an awful tragedy. It had embedded itself three feet into the big Doukabour engine 277 that was attached to the freight train. The freight train was travelling at the time at about 25 miles an hour, and the express was speeding along at the rate of between forty and fifty miles."[27]

The term "Doukabor" was used by Intercolonial men to describe the 2-8-0 Consolidation locomotives typically assigned to heavy freight work. The origin of the name is obscure, but may be related to the hard-work ethic of the Doukabor immigrants from Russia who had settled the Canadian prairies and British Columbia in the late 1800s.

William Wall's obituary contained in the lengthy *Herald* report offered some details that would connect him to the supernatural story of the Cobequid Road ghost. Born at Salmon River, near Truro Nova Scotia, Wall was about 50 years old when he died, and had been a locomotive engineer for almost 35.[28] He lived with his widowed sister, Sarah McDowell[29], in Halifax. She had lost her husband at Windsor Junction "some years ago." In the course of his career, and his involvement with the union, he had been at loggerheads with "some high official" who had ordered the men to quit the union or leave the railway. Wall and his colleagues took their case to Tupper, who not only rescinded the order, but paid the men for the time they were laid off. The "high official" referred to was David Pottinger, then the all-powerful general manager of the Intercolonial at Moncton. The lobby pressed by Wall and his comrades made the engineer something of a hero among his colleagues, if not the public, long before he met his fate at Windsor Junction.

As for Copeland's other victims, the *Daily Herald's* coverage was positively dripping in sympathy for these sober, innocent, and heroic men, but who was William Wall? Two newspapers presented different biographies of the engineer. He was said to have been either fifty or sixty years old; both agreed he was unmarried, from Salmon River, and at the time of his death lived in Halifax with one, or both, of his sisters. Both the Halifax and Moncton newspapers agreed he was a staunch and active member of the Brotherhood of Locomotive Engineers, one who had locked horns with – and bested – the redoubtable minister of railways and canals, Sir Charles Tupper in the past.

So why does his name not appear in the 1901 census? Of the thirteen Walls listed as living in Halifax, county and city, there is not a William among them. Of the twenty Walls listed as residing in Colchester County[30], no William appears. Of the Colchester Walls

Above: The headstone of William Wall and his brother-in-law James McDowell, in Truro's Terrace Hill cemetery.
(Simon Underwood)

living in Truro, Edward Wall was listed as being a fireman, and Judson Wall an engineer, both for the Intercolonial. MacAlpine's Nova Scotia Directory for 1890-97 lists a William Wall as a section man at Riverside, Colchester County , and Malchias Wall as an ICR engineer in Halifax, living on Campbell Road.[31] (Of the twenty-eight Walls listed as living in Moncton at the time of the 1901 census, there is no William among them.) The *MacAlpine's Directory for the City of Halifax* 1900-1901 lists him as an engineer living at 22 Kaye Street in the city.[32]

There is no doubt he was buried in Truro, in what would have been a very public and high profile funeral. William Wall's name appears on a red granite obelisk in Truro's Terrace Hills cemetery, less than two hundred yards from the railway on which he traveled in the course of his career. The inscription indicates he was fifty-four years old, and that he is at rest with his sister, Catherine Wall (died February 7th 1903 aged seventy-seven years) and mother Margaret Wall (died October 29th 1885 aged sixty-one years.)

The most prominent name on the monument, however, is that of another family member, and former Intercolonial Railway employee, James McDowell, who is noted to have been born November 11th 1842, and died March 6th 1890. While the story of his death is not a part of the history of engine No. 239, James McDowell's accident in 1890 is pivotal to the appearance of the Cobequid Road ghost, and that specter's connection to William Wall's death. The Halifax *Chronicle* of February 28th 1890 recounts:

"Conductor James McDowell, of No. 16 freight train, from Truro for Halifax, while stepping from the engine at Windsor Junction about 11:30 yesterday morning fell between the engine and the platform. The rain [sic] being in motion his head was caught by the oil boxes of the wheels and before the train could be stopped his head had been horribly cut and bruised, and other injuries inflicted. When picked up he was unconscious. He was brought to Victoria general hospital. The doctors held a consultation on his case in the afternoon. At midnight the injured man was doing was well as could be hoped for, and it is believed his wounds will not prove fatal."[33]

He died seven days later. McDowell, like his brother-in-law William Wall, was one of the Intercolonial's veterans, and scion of a family with a strong railroading tradition. He was also no stranger to the accidents that occurred at least once in every railroader's life, including the conductor, by whose name the trains were generally known. In his death notice, published in the Halifax *Presbyterian Witness* of Saturday March 8th 1890, it was noted McDowell was "one of the I.C.R.'s oldest employees."[34]

At forty-five years of age, McDowell was certainly younger than a great many members of the train crews. This was also not a true standard of veteran service, for at the time the Intercolonial was only fourteen years old, having opened "officially" between Halifax and Trois Pistoles, Quebec in November of 1876. Some of the employees, however, traced their careers back to the Intercolonial's constituent railways, the Nova Scotia Railway, and the European & North American of New Brunswick, both of which had been established in the mid 1850s and absorbed into the Intercolonial in 1871.

Significant to the career of James McDowell, however, was that he died on the job thirteen years before his brother-in-law met his end near the same station. This made 1903 an especially unhappy year for Sarah (Wall) McDowell (she is identified in the 1881 census.) In February she lost her sister Catherine; in March she observed the anniversary of her husband's death, and in April she lost her brother. If a ghost is the manifestation of an unrequited anguished soul, then surely she is a prime candidate.

The reference in the *Daily Herald* story to "Mrs. McLowell," grieving sister of driver Wall and widow of the man who met his end near the same spot years earlier, almost certainly answers the question of whether or not it is she who is the ghost seen walking the tracks near the Cobequid Road. The sightings began in 2003, one hundred years after the death of her brother, and not her husband, as Darryl Walsh has suggested in *Ghosts of Nova Scotia*.[35]

If William Wall's identity is puzzling, that of his sister is downright mysterious, for there is no record in the 1901 census of any one by the name of McLowell living in Nova Scotia at the time (making the *Herald's* identification an obvious typographical error.) But there are also no Sarah McDowells listed as widows in the census, nor any females by that name of appropriate age, or in residence on Halifax's Duffus Street. Similarly, there are no McDowell widows listed among those of that name in the 1901 census for Truro, nor among the McDowells in the Fall River census district, which included Windsor Junction. There are also no listings for her son, Luther W. McDowell (born in 1875). It may be that she moved from the province with him before the 1901 census, and that the newspaper report of William Wall living with her at the time of his death was incorrect.

Part Three: Human Error, Political Consequences

Whatever fears were being aroused in the minds of the ICR men, the newspapers still sought rational explanations for the Nelson's Pond/Windsor Junction wreck, and were quick to find reasonable causes, and political consequences. Alcohol was the prime suspect, since it was a frequent contributor to many mishaps on the line, as George

R. Stevens has noted in his history of the Intercolonial. Drinking, he claimed went with the "dash and swagger" of life on the road, and for many men raised in "strait-laced homes," a stay at the far end of his division allowed him to "give Old Adam his head."[36] William Wall was no stranger to this often-nomadic life. The 1881 census has him enumerated at Addington in Restigouche County, New Brunswick, living at the home of Daniel O'Keefer.

The Moncton *Daily Times* was among the first to weigh in with accusations against Nelson Copeland of drunkenness and sleeping, made in its April 16th 1903 edition as it reported that Stipendiary Magistrate George Fielding would begin his investigation into the wreck the following day:

"The statement is made openly that Driver Copeland had been drinking heavily. Sometime ago he was reduced from engineer on the freight to a shunter engineer but recently, owing to some influence, was reinstated on the freight. The dead fireman was shovelling coal into the furnace at the moment of the disaster. The brakeman on the engine may have been asleep without violation of rules, his duty being at stake when the train was at the station. Copeland's wife says her husband was subject to fits which reduced him to a comatose condition."[37]

The Halifax *Daily Herald* had offered Fielding some advice and a gesture of restraint in its edition of the previous day, when it claimed "it behooves the magistrate" to ensure the hearing was "very searching and thorough." Noting that Copeland's drinking was openly discussed in the yards around Halifax, the newspaper said the inquiry should be "no half-hearted affair on the part of the magistrate, and it should not be such on the part of the crown or of the public."[38] The *Herald* also introduced an element that Hubbard would have found interesting for his study of the superstitions that ruled the life of the railway man: "It is said that poor Wall remarked, only a day or two before the accident: 'I'm afraid that some of these days I'll meet a train run by men "under the influence," and we'll all be killed.'"[39]

Allied with the drinking rumours was a suggestion that the crew of the Sydney train were asleep, or so weary that could not have noticed their train was approaching Windsor Junction. Several sources told the newspaper that the resting places for men at Richmond (the main yard in Halifax) did not offer "a good chance for sleep." This prompted the *Herald* to suggest Fielding should determine how many hours the crew had been at work and how long their rest period had been.

The Halifax *Chronicle* of the same day provided eyewitness evidence intended to disprove the theory that the demon of alcohol was behind the wreck. Quoting hospital staff, who told the newspaper that Copeland would recover and would soon leave the hospital, the *Chronicle* reported that exhaustion was a more likely cause of the wreck:

"It is in effect that when the big engine drawing number 75 drew near Windsor Junction there were two men in the engine, who through fatigue were unconscious of their surroundings. One was the driver and the other the brakeman. The fireman, who was practically a new man on the road, was hard at work firing. The latter was struck dumb with surprise and fear when he saw the lights at Windsor Junction behind them. He reached over and clutched the driver. The driver was dazed and for a moment or

Above: VIA Rail's west-bound *Ocean* approaches Nelson's Pond, on the Canadian National Railways' Bedford subdivision. This 2006 view is from the path at the new Ashburn Golf Club course. (Andrew Underwood)

two remained in a semi-conscious state. But when he realized the situation he did his best to stop his engine. But it was too late. The crash came a moment or two later. He had done all he could to prevent a collision."[40]

The same source told the newspaper there was "not the least intimation that the driver had been taking intoxicants." In the spirit of competition that has always been healthy for the press, the Halifax *Daily Herald* presented its own evidence to refute the *Chronicle* and indict Copeland on another issue:

"It is said to be a fact that Driver Copeland some time ago was reduced from the position of driver of a freight train to the position of a shunting engineer because of a violation of the rule regarding the use of intoxicants, but that subsequently he was reinstated. He was not a member of the brotherhood of locomotive engineers, so that some other 'pull' got him back."[41]

Just where Copeland had found his "pull," or who exerted it on his behalf, was not revealed. The Moncton *Daily Times* raised another legitimate concern, proving that sensationalism was not always at the root of the news media's coverage of such events. Were the trains then being run on the Intercolonial too large to allow for appropriate warning measures to be taken? Noting that Copeland's Train, No. 75 was hauling 87 cars, the newspaper repeated the claim that bell cords were not workable over such lengths, and if Conductor Hanes and his rear man, Brakeman Murdock McDonald, had noticed the failure to stop as ordered, they were "hopelessly cut off from communications with the locomotive."[42]

The *Times* also wondered if the half-mile length of Copeland's train was too long and heavy for the grades and curves of what are now CN's Bedford and Springhill subdivisions. It was pointed out that the Canadian Pacific Railway, prior to introducing similar large engines on its lines, had engaged in the large-scale replacement of track, and adjustment of curves and grades to suit the new power. All the Intercolonial Railway management did "was to strengthen a few bridges." The question was also asked if the five men assigned to Copeland's run were enough for such a large train.[43]

The notion that Copeland was receiving special favours, as the *Herald* had intimated, reached the floor of Parliament, prompting a response from Andrew Blair, the Liberal minister of railways, and sparking an immediate controversy. In its April 17th edition, the Moncton *Daily Times* reported:

"During the discussion in Parliament on Wednesday night in regard to the prevalence of railway accidents, Mr. Blair, referring to driver Copeland, said: 'That officer was one of the best and most experienced men we had; he had been 32 or 33 years in the service without a mark against him. It appears that he did not lose his life, and he has made the statement that he must have lost his senses, which is the only likely explanation he can make. He knew he was to stop, and was apparently thoroughly alive to the duty of his stopping the train until he came near the point where it was to stop, and then the mental machinery failed to work.'"[44]

The reference to "mental machinery" may have been intended as an allusion to Copeland's alleged insanity, but by finding fault with some of Blair's other "facts," notably about Copeland's age, the anti-Liberal *Times* noted:

"...it is well known among the railway men that within a few months he was suspended on account of drinking and reduced from driver on a regular freight to engineer of a shunting engine in the yard at Truro. He has everything but a good record. He is well known among the railway men who worked with him as a hard drinker and there is not a doubt in their minds as to the cause of the accident, and why he was reinstated after being suspended for cause and placed in charge of a fast train, or any train for that matter, is a question of some importance. Perhaps it is another instance of the ascendancy of the 'political' over the 'practical' management."[45]

The *Times*' statement on Copeland's age is borne out in the 1901 census; he was born in 1863. To underline the venality that often accompanied such incidents, the *Times* could not resist firing a shot at its provincial competitor, the government-friendly Saint John *Telegraph*, whose mission it was " to say 'Yea' to everything that Mr. Blair says."[46]

The *Herald* didn't wait for Fielding's findings. In its May 12th edition, the newspaper triumphantly noted that Copeland, having given his statement from his hospital bed to investigators for the Intercolonial, supported the newspaper's claim that the train's bell cord was faulty. Copeland swore under oath, contrary to the claims of his colleagues, that "was perfectly sober and never was a drinking man."[47] He also contradicted his

Above: Locomotive 239 on the track at Oxford Junction in 1904, where engineer James MacAuley died in the last recorded wreck of the "hoodooed" engine.
(Robert W. Tennant Jr. collection)

wife's claim when he swore "he was not subject to fits and never took one in his life." What Copeland did tell the magistrate – and he had been allowed sufficient time to read the accounts in the local press – was that he had been on the boiler of the locomotive to fix the whistle cord, and he was struck by something, perhaps steam, and rendered unconscious.[48]

Whether or not police magistrate Fielding believed Copeland's denial of ever having suffered from fits (which flew in the face of his wife's statements to the press immediately after the accident) was academic. The federal authorities had launched their own investigation, and just six days later (May 18th) the *Herald* was reporting that Copeland, conductor Haynes, and hostler Norman Purcell of Richmond yard had been dismissed; Copeland for being drunk, Haynes for not knowing Copeland was drunk, and Purcell for knowing Copeland was drunk, but did not warn Haynes.[49] The dismissals did not mollify some critics. There were several calls in the press to have Copeland charged with murder (the Saint John *Sun* called Copeland's crime one of "treason" against his co-workers), but he was permitted to fade into ignominy; whatever political pull he may have had apparently was not sufficient to save him this time.

Writing in The *Maritime Express*, H.B. Jefferson (under the pseudonym J.B. King) noted legal action was instituted against Copeland, but after discharge from hospital he was not molested and was allowed to "exit quietly" to the United States.[50] Jefferson noted the reason might have been to save the government from any further embarrassment, by having to admit that the Intercolonial did not allow sufficient rest time for its train crews or that the men were forced to work "atrociously long hours." The authorities were not anxious "to have the labor delinquencies of a government road aired in court."[51]

Above: Via Rail's *Ocean* approaches Oxford Junction, where the railway used to branch off to Oxford and Pugwash, near the site of the wreck that killed engineer James MacAuley. (Jay Underwood)

In any event, engine No. 239 was retrieved from the wreckage, restored at the Moncton shops, and sent back out on the line. In the meantime, Jefferson notes, the locomotive's reputation was preceding it, the Truro *Headlight* and the Moncton *Times* both referring to "The Hoo-doo 239," a name that would follow the engine forever.[52]

At this point, however, Jefferson's history becomes faulty. He notes:

"The 239 was not long out of the shops again before she had another sharp run-in, but this time without serious casualties. One dark, stormy night a heavy gale blew a box car out on the main line at the west end of Truro yard, right on to the pilot of 239, this time with another celebrated old time runner, Jim MacAulay, of Stellarton and Moncton, in the cab – the only man who ever rode her into a collision and walked away unhurt."[53]

As the Halifax *Daily Herald* of November 3rd 1904 will note, however, this accident occurred "several years" before the Windsor Junction wreck and before No. 239 came into service. In the meantime, No. 239 was involved in another wreck.

Part Four: The Inevitable Question

The superstitious among the Intercolonial men were already becoming wary of service on engine No. 239, but the notion of "hoodoo" became a fixed fact in many minds after the wreck of November 1st 1904 at Oxford Junction. The Halifax *Daily*

Herald could no longer ignore the supernatural implications of the engine's history, asking the inevitable question in its November 3rd edition:

"Is Intercolonial Railway locomotive 239 "hoodooed?" is a question that is being asked in railway circles. Three of her former engineers are in the grave – Samuel Trider and William Wall, and one killed north of Moncton – the result of accidents that have befallen her during her unlucky career, extending over a period of a little over two years, and her latest victim, Engineer James McAuley, succumbed to his injuries, while Fireman W. C. Lawrence is seriously injured, as the result of an accident that occurred at Oxford Junction Tuesday, in which the locomotive was prominent."[54]

The report noted that engineer McAuley had had a narrow escape for his life several years earlier while running the same train during the severe gale and thunderstorm of which Jefferson had written.[55] It should be pointed out that this previous accident, while involving the same train, did not necessarily include the same locomotive, as Jefferson had supposed.

James McAuley was buried in Moncton's Elmwood Cemetery. He was fifty-four years old and a native of Ireland. He married Lois A.C. Riley in 1877, and they had five children, three sons and two daughters. He had been at the throttle in a wreck close to Christmas in 1902, although there is no indication from the newspaper report of December 29th if No. 239 had been at the head of that train.[56]

In the aftermath of the November 1904 wreck, the *Herald* and the *Times* were quick to tally up engine No. 239's ghastly toll[57] , but neither took the obvious step of adding McAuley to the list, perhaps an indication that journalists, with their grasp of the technical issues, were still somewhat reluctant to toy with superstition or fate: McCauley, this man of "splendid character,"[58] had become engine No. 239's thirteenth victim. He had joined Trider, Kennedy, McDonald, McLean, Toole, the first William Wall, Minnie Croke, the second William Wall, Oakley, Thorpe, Hill and the unknown engineer north of Moncton. The "hoodoo" was complete – the numbers did not lie – for as Hubbard noted, thirteen was of special significance to railroaders: "Many refuse to handle a number 13, or begin a run on Friday the 13th, or have anything to do with 13."[59]

But the tally is suspicious, because of the lack of detail surrounding the wreck alleged to have occurred "north of Moncton." It is odd that neither the *Herald*, nor the Moncton newspapers, usually so assiduous in their accounts of the deaths of local railway men, omitted the name of the engineer supposedly killed "north of Moncton." The chronology suggests this wreck occurred sometime between the Belmont and Windsor Junction calamities, yet no details can be found in any of the three newspapers. Perhaps this was a case of hysteria pervading the story, for the public of the time was becoming quite attuned to the supernatural.

The concept of "hoodoo" was then popular in North America, although it was typically misunderstood and misrepresented. It came to public notice about 1891, largely through the blues music emanating from New Orleans. Blues also leaned heavily on railroad themes for its lyrics, so the association was easily made. While it quickly came to be synonymous with the spirit world and the supernatural, the word "hoodoo" had actually been introduced into the United States by the African slaves, and properly describes various forms of African-based systems of magic, spiritual and medicinal healing, and "hexing," via the use of primarily roots and herbs.[60] The definitions then became as confused as those commonly associated with "voodoo," coming to mean something believed to bring bad luck, a charm believed to embody magical powers, or a malevolent source of misfortune.

This inappropriate use of the word isn't the only portent of misfortune attached to locomotive No. 239. While fear of the number thirteen has been traced to early Christian, and even earlier Nordic mythology, the morbid fear of the number wasn't identified, or named (triskaidekaphobia) until Boston-based psychoanalyst Isadore H. Coriat published *Abnormal Psychology* in 1911, when the paranormal and supernatural again seized the public's imagination (the word's etymology is Greek, from tris, "three", kai, "and", deka, "ten" (making thirteen), plus phobia, "fear, flight".) Lately triskaidekaphobia has come to mean the fear of Friday the 13th. Even in this, however, locomotive No. 239 can lay claim to an eerie connection.[61]

Recently, 1998 was one of those rare years in which Friday the 13th occurs three times. Every year has at least one Friday the 13th, but in each of the 28-year cycles of the calendar there are four years that have three such dates. In the year that No. 239 was built there was only one Friday the 13th; so too in 1904 – but in 1903, there were three: in February, March and November, and numerologists might consider it significant that the numbers of that year, 1-9-0 and 3 all add up to thirteen. Certainly the number thirteen didn't prevent the management of the Intercolonial Railway from tempting fate. Train 13 (Halifax-Truro by the 1909 timetable) left North Street station at 13:15 daily except Sunday, a milk-run stopping at all nineteen stations between the two points.

There were, however, less otherworldly factors at play in No. 239's wrecks, something many of the newspapers of the day overlooked – the sheer physical and metal strain of the work. There was some appreciation for the driver's lot. As early as August of 1890, the Woodstock, New Brunswick, *Carleton Sentinel* sent a reporter along for a ride and first-hand experience. The journalist noted that his midnight ride gave him "some idea of the hazard, the nervous strain, the grinding anxiety attendant upon the locomotive engineer."[62] By the turn of the century this "nervous strain" was steadily increasing as more trains were added to the Intercolonial schedule, to reflect the growing popularity of the train as the transportation of choice. In June of 1900, the Halifax *Chronicle* reported that the increase in traffic – because of the boom at the new Sydney steel mills and coal mines, and the increased tourist trade – made additional trains desirable. "To Truro there will be eight trains a day, to Saint John, Pictou and New Glasgow, three trains, and to Sydney two trains daily."[63] The newspaper did not attach any significance to the news that there would be thirteen trains a day leaving Halifax under the new schedule.[64] These increasing schedules were capable of wreaking havoc on every member of the on-board crew, from driver to conductor, and to those responsible for the control of the traffic.

Part Five: Changing Numbers, Changing Fortunes

According to Jefferson, locomotive 239 had quickly become a "railroad pariah," although he had admitted to not being able to recall the details of all the "other wrecks the details of which escape me now, and innumerable lesser accidents which helped to keep a lively fear of her green."[65] He did note that some engineers refused to have anything to do with the locomotive, calling in sick, trading shifts, anything to avoid having to take the throttle.

Not even the report of ghostly apparitions in the cab of No. 239, however, could do much to deter engineers from taking the locomotive out on runs, for the engine stayed in service long after the report became public. Competition for driving jobs proved to be a greater force than superstition about ghosts, for despite the dangers, the position as an engineer on the government-owned railway was highly coveted among the ranks of the staff, and drivers were considered the aristocracy of the working class. Much of the status was due to the effort it took to reach the position (unless one enjoyed the apparent political "pull" of a Nelson Copeland!) Gairns offers an insight into the career path of the locomotive driver, noting that advancement through the ranks often meant having to serve time on the footplate of an engine "that is cordially disliked by every one who has anything to do with it."[66]

This "cordial dislike" could always be countered with a timely renumbering of the locomotive stud, as the railway amalgamated or reorganized its rosters to allow new engines into the fold. Hubbard notes:

"…Plenty of engines have been renumbered to get rid of a stigma. The Erie's 2917, for instance, had been in a series of accidents in which crew men were killed and was generally regarded as a hoodoo until the company obligingly renumbered her 2945, which is her number today." [67]

Was it to allay superstitious fears, or to assuage some necessity of administration that engine No. 239 was renumbered IRC 629 in January of 1912? Certainly the locomotive stayed with the railway as it underwent its metamorphosis into to what became known as Canadian National Railways, first re-designated Canadian Government Railways engine No. 629 in January of 1915, and later renumbered and re-designated Canadian National Railways 1542 on September 1st 1919.[68] The nine disappeared from the number boards, but remained in the date of its final transformation.

September was a particularly auspicious month for the railroad fraternity, as Hubbard has noted, being the ninth month of the calendar.[69] He also pointed out that the first ever railway fatality occurred in that month in 1830, when Member of Parliament William Huskisson ventured from his railway car to that carrying then-Prime Minister the Duke of Wellington, only to be run down by George Stevenson's locomotive Rocket!

It appeared the hoodoo locomotive could not escape its fate, and yet the engine was carried along, without further incident, as it was superheated and re-geared at Moncton in February of 1923, and finally retired and scrapped at the former Intercolonial shops there June 6th 1936.

It would be convenient for the story to suggest the hoodoo was removed from engine No. 239 by some act of witchcraft or exorcism – such as that employed in April of 1955 to remove an ancient Mi'kmaq curse from the then-new Macdonald bridge in Halifax – but these later alterations tend to prove there was something far less than supernatural about the accidents that plagued No. 239.

The Dickson locomotive entered service with the Intercolonial in the twilight years of the "Ten Wheeler" type's use as an express engine. Writing in the *Canadian Government Railway Employees Magazine*, G. E. McCoy, a draftsman at the Moncton Shops noted the "Pacific" type (4-6-2) engines were replacing the "Ten Wheelers." Once introduced, the Intercolonial was quick to accept the advantages of the bigger, more powerful locomotives:

"...Pacific type locomotives were first used in the United States in 1902; in 1904, two years later, the Intercolonial Railway, realizing the necessity of securing larger and more efficient passenger locomotives, placed an order with the Canadian Locomotive Company, Kingston, for twelve Pacific Type locomotives, – these were delivered early in 1905 and were the first locomotives of this type to be built in Canada. The satisfactory service rendered by them led to the placing of orders in 1906, 1908 and 1911 for more locomotives of the same type and size."[70]

Once again, as McCoy inadvertently noted, the Intercolonial proved its managers weren't afraid of unlucky numbers:

"In service these locomotives are quite often hauling fast passenger trains composed of 2-Postal, 3-Baggage, 1-Second-Class, 2-First-Class, 1-Dining and 4-Sleeping Cars, making a total of 13 cars and weighing from 600 to 700 tons, exclusive of engine and tender, over the mountains on 1% grades."[71]

Passenger express service itself became a less fatal proposition when the railway began using steel cars, forsaking the lighter wooden cars that had suffered so badly in all of No. 239's wrecks. Writing in the employees' magazine of June 1915, McCoy noted it was not until 1902 that the use of metal was given serious consideration.[72] So it was that engine No. 239, and dozens like it, were removed from the prestige of the express runs, and relegated to "suburban" passenger trains or light freight duty. On these slower tasks, there was less likelihood of calamity occurring.

At the same time that No. 239 was being renumbered, the railway, now called Canadian Government Railways (CGR), was moving toward a system that allowed drivers to become better acquainted with the operating "quirks" of their locomotives – recall that neither Samuel Trider nor William Wall were that well acquainted with No. 239 when they met their fate. In the December 1914 edition of the *CGR employees' magazine*, it was noted that the engines in use on the line between Chaudière Junction and Montreal were the first to become "assigned engines," with specific crews rostered to man each unit.[73] The General Master Mechanic, W.U. Appleton was "highly pleased" with the results, which included a decrease in oil and fuel consumption, and an increased pride being taken by the crews of the locomotives in their care. This system has been dropped in today's diesel locomotive era.

At the time, other employees quickly endorsed this new operating procedure. In the July 1915 edition of the magazine W. B. Scott, Chief Clerk and Master Mechanic at Campbellton, New Brunswick, wrote that the system of running "pool" locomotives meant the same engineer and firemen were seldom together for two trips in succession, and were unfamiliar not only with the quirks of the locomotive, but with the manner in which each other drove, or fired an engine:

"Each locomotive has different parts that require more or less special attention and watching. Therefore an engineer starting out with an engine with which he is not familiar and a fireman with whom he has not been running for some time, must

Above: VIA Rail's *Ocean*, outward bound from Halifax in 2000, goes over the crossing at Cobequid Road, near Windsor Junction, where the ghost of a forlorn Sarah McDowell has most been sighted. (Jay Underwood)

operate the engine for some distance before he learns what parts of the engine need careful attention as well as the methods employed by the fireman. When all these are considered together it can be seen that on the first part of the run the crew is not as efficient as it would be otherwise and become tired out much quicker than would seem necessary."[74]

According to Scott, this led to a tendency to make the fireman neglect cleaning his part of the cab and the headlight while meeting trains or standing in the sidings, and since he did not expect to be on the engine again for some time, he did not bother to clean at all, given the several hours of hard work ahead of him. This same condition applied to the engineer – who had his side of the cab to maintain:

"The result is that the engine is not in as good a state of repair or is not nearly as clean, and as everybody is running the engine nobody in particular can be held responsible for the dirty condition. The small repair jobs are not done, as it is not to be expected that the Roundhouse staff could find them as could the engineer."[75]

This final state of affairs could explain why, for example, Samuel Trider did not stop and inspect his locomotive's damaged pilot before taking it out on its fatal run to Belmont. Scott suggested that before the system of assigned locomotives went into effect, it was quite common for an engineer to give up his train on account of some part breaking. Under the new system, it was understood that a disabled engine would, in almost every case, mean lost time for the crew.[76]

Scott also points to an explanation for why driver Nelson Copeland might have been asleep at the throttle of his engine when it struck No. 239 at Windsor Junction/Nelson's Pond:

"The engineer on arriving at the terminal is usually tired out and does not give the engine the same careful inspection that he would if he knew that he was going out on the same engine again and knew that he would be held responsible if this engine did not make reasonable mileage and be in good condition."[77]

Anyone not given to beliefs in superstition, flights of fancy or the supernatural, would conclude that engine No. 239's unhappy history was the result of bad luck, bad management and the randomness of fate. But of all the locomotives the Intercolonial had on its roster, none had the record of No. 239, and no other had the railway workers talking darkly of "hoodoo."

Jefferson notes that nearly all the engines of the 234-239 series had plenty of mishaps, especially 234 and 237. The latter was involved in as many bad spills as 239, notably a serious wreck at Grand Lake, and a fatal headon [sic] crash between the eastbound CPR and the *Midnight Express* at the Polly Bog, near Brookfield in 1907.[78] The inevitable suspicion arising from the many wrecks of No. 239 and its sister locomotives is that they suffered from some design or manufacturing flaw. The Intercolonial Dickson Ten-Wheelers of 1902 (numbers 234 to 239) were known as "Big Dicksons." They were fast engines, with 72-inch drivers – among the largest on the Intercolonial. The boilers were high mounted (nine feet two inches to the smoke-box center line), about a foot higher than on other Ten-Wheelers. The high centre of gravity would make them more prone to rollover on curves, but most of the Intercolonial accidents involved head-on collisions or sideswipes, where this aspect of the engine design could not have been a factor.

By comparison, the Maine Central (MEC) – described by George Drury as being a "Ten-Wheeler road" (in the twentieth century MEC had 67 Ten-Wheelers built, more than twice as many as any other road engine on the roster) – never used any Ten-Wheelers with drivers greater than 67 inches.[79] These were the O-3 class engines of 1918, and the original O-Class engines of 1903-1905 only had 64-inch drivers. Both these types were considered large for their day, and both were used for freight and local passenger service.

Certainly there were those in the public arena who wanted to disparage and find fault with the American-built engines. When Railways Minister A.G. Blair placed the first orders in 1900, the opposition rebuked him for overlooking both the capacity of the Moncton shops and the Kingston, Ontario locomotive works to fill the orders, accusing him of using cheaper American-built locomotives in order to ensure the Intercolonial would show a small surplus on its capital accounts.

The Moncton *Transcript*, locked in its own battle with the *Times* of that city, placed some of the blame on the employees at the Moncton shops. In its March 14th 1900 edition it accused "certain employees" of placing obstacles in the way of the New Brunswick plant's getting contracts that were going to Kingston.[80] In its March 17th edition, the newspaper expanded on its criticism of the workers, and the *Times*, which had linked the orders to the electioneering then taking place. Noting that four locomotives had been built in Moncton, the *Transcript* reminded its readers that the *Times* had been less than enthusiastic: "not one word of commendation came from our contemporary. Sneers were its reward."[81] Furthermore, the *Transcript* said, the men of the Moncton shops were not encouraged to accept more locomotive building because the shops would then be expected to operate under the same less-than generous conditions that the Kingston workers endured, in order to ensure the bids were competitive.

In typical Canadian fashion, a compromise was reached, with an order for four locomotives to be built at Moncton, but this was almost automatically seen to be a government condemnation of the quality of the work at Kingston. The political furor continued to swirl about the perceived slight to Kingston's reputation, especially when the plant closed its doors. In this the *Transcript* found an ally in Ontario. In its October 6th edition of the same year the newspaper reported that because Kingston had closed its doors, Railway Minister A.G. Blair had been obliged to order more engines from the United States:

"The truth is the Kingston Locomotive Works have been crippled for the want of capital rather than the want of orders. Indeed the *Transcript* understands that the Minister of Railways offered to give them sufficient orders to keep the works running. But the Kingston works did not possess sufficient capital to carry on great undertakings, and this fact alone forced them to close down until other arrangements could be made with capitalists."[82]

Quoting the Kingston, Ontario, *Times and Independent*, the *Transcript* pointed out that had Kingston been able to build engines at prices that were competitive with Baldwin in Philadelphia, the Ontario plant would have received more orders. Again a compromise was reached, after the Kingston plant found new capitalists ready to infuse new life into the works.

The ill-will that had permeated Canadian railway politics since the Intercolonial was conceived lingered for some time, and it is reasonable to assume that opponents of the American-built engines would use any opportunity to impugn the quality and reliability.

The notion of the "hoodoo" could have been nothing more than a convenient political device invented by Charles Manning of the Moncton *Times*, or of Lunn, of the Truro *Headlight*.

The Intercolonial certainly had its full complement of adversaries in 1904, provoked in no small measure by Railways Minister Henry R. Emmerson's bold introduction of a crack new Halifax-Montreal passenger express service – The *Ocean* – at a time when the railway was incurring high deficits. Telling the House of Commons he was determined to make the Intercolonial the "great asset of the Dominion," Emmerson defended the cost increases over the first ten months of 1904, noting most of it went to increased wages for employees.

Emmerson's deficit followed a small surplus in 1903, and the minister noted another large increase in costs was in keeping equipment up to standard, making the railway safer for passengers and freight. His estimate showed that for the first ten months of 1904, these costs would amount to more than $600,000.[83] Significant in that amount was the estimate of cost of repairs to locomotives. Engine No. 239's repairs alone would consume the lion's share of the $26,427 set aside for that purpose.

It went without saying that the improvements planned by Emmerson would also make the railway a safer operation, but his arguments enraged his opponents and their supporters in the daily press. At that point any flaw in the railway's operation would become a weapon to be used against the government, perhaps even the far-fetched notion that a "hoodoo" plagued one American-built locomotive.

It must be asked, however, how random could No. 239's fate have been, given the eerie recurrence of the unlucky numbers associated with its misfortunes? With no definite answers, engine No. 239 must pass into history forever trailing its mysterious past behind. For the railway men and others who met their end at its throttle, perhaps the only fitting epitaph is the anonymous poem:

> Until the brakes are turned on time,
> Life's throttle valve shut down,
> He wakes to pilot in the crew
> That wears the martyr's crown.
> On schedule time on upper grade
> Along the homeward section,
> He lands his train at God's roundhouse
> The morn of resurrection.
> His time all full, no wages docked,
> His name on God's payroll,
> And transportation through to Heaven
> A free pass for his soul.[84]

CHAPTER 2

The Harbour Bridge Curse

Three times a bridge over these waves shall rise,
built by the pale face, so strong and wise,
three times shall fall like a dying breath,
in storm, in silence, and last in death.[1]

- Alleged Mi'kmaq curse on the Halifax bridges

IF the "hoodoo" of Locomotive No. 239 was not the invention of a newspaper with a political axe to grind, the Halifax bridge curse certainly was.

The real powers of hoodoo, hexes and curses find their strength in the willingness of the victim to believe in them. The notion of having been "cursed" can often lead to a person making wholesale changes in his life and character in order to avoid incurring the promised penalty. As Dr. Robert Todd Carroll, a philosophy instructor with the Sacramento City College's department of philosophy notes, "a curse is a prayer or invocation expressing a wish that harm, misfortune, injury, great evil, etc., be brought upon another person, place, thing, clan, nation, etc. People are also said to be cursed if harm comes to them regularly or in seeming disproportion to the rest of us."[2]

"Belief in curses may make it easier to explain why bad things often happen to good people: they are cursed because of some bad thing an ancestor did. A little bit of reflection, however, should reveal that this is not a very satisfactory explanation. Whether it is God or Nature doing the cursing, neither seems very just in punishing the children for the sins of their mothers or fathers."[3]

While most curses seem to be cast upon people – either individually or in groups – the willingness to inflict evil is not limited to the living. The Hope and Koh-i-noor diamonds, the jewels of French and British royalty, were believed to have been cursed, and Indian curses are deeply engrained in the folklore of New England. One such curse was cast over an entire community, as William James Sidis (writing as Charles Edward Beals Jr.) has recorded. Sidis' history refers to the New Hampshire community of Burton, once known as Chocorua, after a local native chief. The chief met his end at the hands of settler Cornelius Campbell, and tradition claims that the dying man's last act was to curse all white men, praying to his gods that disease would strike their crops and cattle:

"The cattle did indeed sicken and die, it being impossible to raise a calf. And even robust men seemed to waste away. There was something wrong, something that could not be accounted for. Quickly the superstitious fear that the Indian's curse was in effect

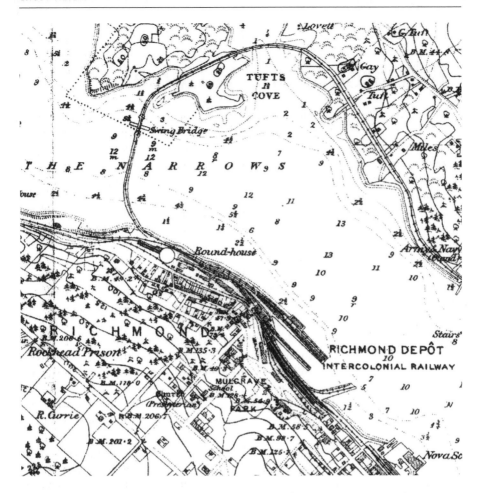

Above: Detail from an old Imperial War Department chart of 1897, showing the location of the Intercolonial Railway bridge across The Narrows.
(Jay Underwood collection)

crept over the minds of these hardy frontiersmen. With such a handicap Burton did
not grow as fast as the surrounding towns."[4]

Such Indian curses are believed to be exceptionally potent, as witnessed by the
so-called "Curse of Tecumseh" that describes a chain of events beginning with the
death from pneumonia of United States President William Henry Harrison in 1841.
Commonly attributed to the chief Tecumseh – or his brother Tenskwatawa (also known
as The Prophet) – who was defeated in the Battle of Tippecanoe by Harrison, this curse
is said to have proclaimed the death of all presidents elected every twenty years.

Some versions of the story indicate that Tecumseh's mother pronounced the curse
when Tecumseh died. The coincidental twenty-year pattern was noted in the 1934

edition of *Ripley's Believe It or Not.*[5] Among the victims of that curse were presidents Harrison (elected 1840), Lincoln (1860), Garfield (1880), McKinley (1900), Harding (1920), Roosevelt (1940) and Kennedy (1960). Only presidents Ronald Reagan (1980) and George W. Bush (2000) appear to have escaped Tecumseh's wrath, but Reagan was the target of several assassination attempts.

It should then come as no surprise to learn of the apparent longevity of a curse placed upon a bridge or crossing of water, especially in Nova Scotia and especially when it involves the native Mi'kmaw. So it was with the legend of the curse placed upon the Halifax Harbour bridges. Mi'kmaq folklorist Catherine Martin of the Millbrook Band near Truro, Nova Scotia notes there are at least four versions of origin of the legend.

The first version, found in the records of the Nova Scotia Archives and Records Management Service (NSARMS), complete with a poem, speaks about a European who was having an affair with a married Indian woman. The woman stole off into the night for their assignation. And was followed by her husband, down to the shores of the Narrows on Bedford Basin: "He was very upset and followed as they got into a canoe. He snuck up on them and attempted to kill the pale face, but instead killed his wife with his hatchet. He was so distraught that he cursed the pale face and said never shall they cross this water again."[6] Typical of many such legends, however, are the variations on the same theme, as Martin has noted. The second version of this story involves a British naval officer who was seeing the wife of a chief, whom she left for the British officer. The cuckolded husband also discovered them, and a similar curse was cast.[7]

The third version again involves a competition for a forbidden native woman and two braves who competed for her favour. The maiden chose to marry the wealthier of the two men, and as she prepared herself for her wedding day on the shores of the Bedford Basin, the unsuccessful suitor crept down and killed her, escaping across the water and preventing pursuit by cutting loose all the canoes. The canoes had been tied together as a makeshift bridge across the basin, and other braves cursed the waters so that no-one could cross them again.[8] The final version, as Martin notes, is quite specific about the characters, but – contrary to the best oral traditions – vague on names. It claims that the maiden in question was stolen from her father by a European sea captain, and the distraught chief cursed the waters so that no man could cross them in safety again.[9]

Interviewed for the thirtieth anniversary of the opening of Halifax's Angus L. Macdonald bridge in 1985, bridge commission manager Gerry Kay was quoted in the *Chronicle-Herald* of April 1st 1985 (no particular significance is attached to the date in this case) as saying the amorous sailor in the second and perhaps fourth versions noted by Martin was a lieutenant by the name of Smith, who had gone ashore to get water from the Sackville River for the crew of his ship. This incident is supposed to have occurred in the 1700s, and could not have been before 1749, when Cornwallis arrived.[10] This version bears a striking and perhaps convenient similarity to the legend of Pocahontas, the Virginian girl, daughter of the Algonquian chief Powhatan, who saved the life of Captain John Smith. (The Mi'kmaq are an Algonquian tribe.)

The most immediate clue in favour of supporting the idea that the curse has no validity, however, is the conflict it poses with Mi'kmaq culture. Dan Paul of Millbrook, Nova Scotia, an historian of his people's oral tradition, has suggested the curse was the figment of a white man's imagination. Chief Paul says such a curse would have been contrary to Mi'kmaq cultural values, which mandated "that one help others, not try to harm them."[11] This misunderstanding of Mi'kmaq values is in keeping with a key theme of Paul's book *We were not the Savages*, and his supplementary website, that native Americans were victimized by dehumanizing and demonizing colonial propaganda:

"British officialdom, to keep English Subjects suitably aroused against the Eastern Amerindians, blamed them for a good many of the crimes – they used the term 'outrages' in their reports – committed in their colonies. In the case of the Mi'kmaq, without evidence, they blamed them for all the so-called 'outrages' that occurred in Acadia. [As Nova Scotia was known at the time of the alleged affair between Smith and the maiden.]"[12]

The Halifax curse, if it existed at that time, didn't seem to have much of an influence, for in 1796 – less than fifty years after it was supposed to have been cast – Jonathan Tremaine, a wealthy Dartmouth flour mill owner, was granted a ninety-nine-year lease for his newly-formed Halifax Bridge Company, to build a span across the harbour.[13] Tremaine planned to finance the toll bridge by selling shares, but the plan came to nothing, although no curse appears to have been involved. Rather, it may have been due – according to one history of Dartmouth – to a failure in the Nantucket whaling industry, which had set up a station on the Dartmouth shore. Tremaine and his Nantucket compatriots were among the first settlers in the community, but with the whaling industry in trouble, his pool of potential investors quickly dwindled. He would later become a trustee of the Dartmouth Commons, and a patron of Christ Church,

Below: The bridge across The Narrows, showing the volume of traffic often placed upon it. (Nova Scotia Archives and Records Management Service N-98)

one of the first houses of worship in the town.[14] Nor did the thought of impending disaster stop the Tremaines from investing in the harbour ferry business. In 1815 Jonathan Tremaine Jr, and John Tremaine were among the incorporators of the Halifax Steam Boat Company, which launched the first of the regularly scheduled ferries.[15]

Tremaine's lack of success may have contributed somewhat to the delay in the second attempt to build a bridge, for it was not until April 14th of 1845 that an act of the legislature (Bill 71) formed a second private company. The Richmond Bridge Company was incorporated by John Edward Starr and Arthur Wellington Godfrey to build a toll bridge across the harbour. The promoters also sought a loan from the provincial treasury to finance their project, and were given a time limit of three years in which to make their plan work. Failing that, the act of incorporation would be rescinded. It was rescinded, but that did not mark the end of the Starr family's involvement.

The much longed for bridge was built by the Intercolonial Railway in 1886, and one might have expected the Halifax bridge curse legend to gain currency in 1893 when the bridge collapsed for the second time. The unfortunate history of the Intercolonial's branch line from Halifax to Dartmouth has been told succinctly by Mrs. William Lawson, (Mary Jane Katzman). The line was built in 1886, covering the six miles from Richmond to the Woodside Sugar Refinery. The bridge crossed at the Narrows, and the rails followed the shore to Woodside, where a harbour ferry now lands. The bridge measured 198 metres (650 feet), and was built in water from eighteen to twenty-three metres (sixty to seventy-five feet) deep. M.J. Hogan of Quebec was the contractor and builder of the woodwork; Dartmouth's Starr Manufacturing Company provided the iron superstructure of the drawbridge, and Duncan Waddell of Dartmouth built the stonework erected in water twelve metres (forty feet) deep. The branch opened January 6th 1886, and a train left every morning for Richmond to connect with the Intercolonial Railway. Another train turned in the evening to the station at Dartmouth with passengers or freight.[16]

Strangely, Mrs. Lawson's editor treats the devastating collapse of the bridge as a footnote:

"This bridge, with the exception of the "draw" and one or two other portions, was swept away during a terrible wind and rain storm on the night of 7th September, 1891. It had been erected upon crib-work piers, filled with stone, to which were bolted the piles and other superstructure. This plan had been adopted, because the engineer, it is said, had reported that the piles could not penetrate the bottom. After the destruction of the work, the contract of rebuilding it was given to Connor of Moncton. Engineers again made an examination of the bottom, and this time they reported it to be partially soft. The crib-work plan was abandoned, and piles were driven directly into the soil. This second structure was completed about January 1892. It must, however, have been extremely unstable for about two o'clock on Sunday morning, 23rd July, 1893, with hardly a breath of air moving, the greater part of the bridge from the draw to the Halifax shore, was carried away. A train had crossed about six hours before. After the second destruction, a strong effort was made to have the railway brought directly to Dartmouth without crossing the harbour."[17]

The first collapse during the cyclone of 1891 elicited no references to Mi'kmaq curses, as one might have suspected. Indeed, the local coverage was quite muted. The Halifax

Herald carried no mention of the loss of the bridge until its edition of September 11th, and that was merely a report reprinted from the *Mail,* consisting of one paragraph.

Unfortunately copies of the *Mail* from that era are not readily available, but it did not appear that the event was treated as cataclysmic; the weekly *NovaScotian* carried only two paragraphs in its September 12th edition:

"In Dartmouth a good deal of damage was done. In several places the railway track is twisted and the roadbed washed away. Trees in all parts of the town were uprooted and the ground is strewn with broken branches. All the fruit on the trees is blown off....

The Dominion government seems to have fared badly, the Narrows Bridge and the elevator being injured more than any other property. The bridge is injured to an extent that can scarcely be repaired for six months or more. In the meantime the town of Dartmouth will be without railway communication with the outside world."[18]

The Moncton *Daily Times* of September 9th 1891, published in the town that was headquarters to the federally owned railway, focused briefly on the damage to the port, since other areas of the province also suffered from the devastating high winds:

"Yesterday's weather was showery. There was a southwest rainstorm. Late in the evening a cyclone came on. At ten o'clock the wind was blowing thirty miles an hour, and at eleven must have exceeded sixty miles. Much damage was done on land. The telephone service was completely demoralized: shutters, trees, chimneys, fences, etc., were blown down. The cyclone's greatest fury was felt in the harbour. The railway drawbridge at the Narrows was lifted from its foundation and swept down the harbour. Its destruction is a serious loss to the I.C.R. and Dartmouth, as all freight and passenger trains going to and coming from Dartmouth have to be hung up. It will take a year to rebuild it. Four hundred feet of the grain elevator chute was blown down. Schooner J.L. Crosley was sunk at the gashouse wharf. There was $1,500 insurance on the vessel. Schooner Fanny B. was torn from the fastening at the sugar refinery wharf and driven ashore. Schooner Salvador, also at the refinery wharf, had her desk washed away. At the Lorne club the tide did much damage. Bathing houses were swept away and all the small boats smashed. Yacht Lenore dragged her moorings and ran down the yacht Nautilus, carrying away the latter's jib boom and forward gear. At the yacht squadron wharf the Wenonah and Youla came to grief. Both went ashore and are badly damaged. Yacht Hebe, moored in the Arm broke loose and drifted ashore. There is a large hole in the bow."[19]

Whatever may be said about the later bridge, there is little doubt about the quality of the design and construction of the first. It was the work of the Intercolonial Railway engineering department's superintendent Peter Souter Archibald, who had built the suspension bridge over the Saint John River in New Brunswick. He had been on the original staff assisting Sandford Fleming with the construction of the Intercolonial from Truro to Trois Rivières, Quebec. The curved design was intended to enable the span to withstand the strain of winter ice and the ebb and flow of the tide – especially in the spring – as the bridge bore heavy traffic. Starr Manufacturing had previously made its name known for its production of ice skates, but John Forbes, who had designed the central steel swing span, was no novice. He had erected the first steel bridge constructed in the Dominion over the Nine Mile River at Elmsdale in 1875. Previous to this installation, iron and steel bridges had been purchased from the Great Britain and the United States.

A report in the Halifax *Star* of June 6th 1928 noted that Nova Scotia Provincial Museum curator Harry Piers was in the process of gathering information about the former bridge, as "it is reported there is nome [sic] new developments near at hand," and revealed more detail about the second bridge:

"The bridge was built by Oakes and Paw, their contract price being $84,000. The centre circular stone pier on which the steel swing revolved was built by Duncan Waddell, of Dartmouth, his price being $10,000. The steel swing was constructed by the Starr Manufacturing Co. for $19,945. This would make a total cost, exclusive of rails, of $113,945. The swing could be worked by one man. The bridge measured 650 feet in length and was built in water as deep as from 60 to 75 feet."[20]

There is no reference to any curse. The second collapse appeared to confirm the existence of the curse, but may, as Carroll has noted, simply have been a case of confirmation bias. The *Herald* report of July 25th 1893 is far more detailed than that of the disaster two years previously: "About 2 o'clock Sunday morning the Intercolonial railway bridge across the Narrows, connecting the main line of the I.C.R. with the Dartmouth branch collapsed. The western end – by far the greater portion – from near the draw to the Halifax side was carried away. This is the second collapse for the Narrows Bridge."[21] Again, there was no reference to any supposed curse. The report did offer a mild rebuke for the railway's apparent stinginess, noting the bridge was not the best available option. The editor suggested the bridge had been built to satisfy the popular demands of the residents of Dartmouth for an immediate railway connection, but a better connection would have been from Dartmouth to Windsor Junction, without crossing the Basin.

Another connection could have been made by a line from Dartmouth to Musquodoboit and a junction with the Intercolonial at Stewiacke:

"The next best thing to have done would have been to build an iron bridge across the Narrows with stone piers. To do that would have cost about $400,000, and it was decided to be out of the region of possibility in the meantime. So the cheapest method was adopted – to construct a wooden bridge, on piles, from shore to shore, with a draw. That would cost but a small proportion of what it would have taken for the stone and iron structure, but it now looks as though it would have been cheaper in the long run to make the work a permanent one at the start. After two collapses it is not likely the department a third time will depend upon a pile bridge for the important work of bearing across the harbour trains of valuable goods and numbers of human lives."[22]

The threat that a Musquodoboit line presented to Halifax's predominance as the premier port on the nation's Atlantic coast is not made apparent in this article, but a line from Dartmouth to Country Harbour, an even deeper port than Halifax, closer to England, could have resulted in Halifax becoming a secondary station. This proposal had been considered in Major William Robinson's 1848 report.

The *Herald* then went into the most concise history of the construction of the first bridge that had been done before, or since:

"The first bridge differed from the second in the manner of its construction, though both were built on piles. When the bridge was decided upon engineers were sent to make examinations of the bottom. As a result of their borings they first reported that there was a rock bottom, impenetrable to piles. Orders were therefore given to build crib work for a certain distance up, and upon that bolt the piles and construct wooden trestlework to the surface and above. On top of that were laid the longitudinal beams, and the sleepers bearing the rails. The crib work was filled in with stones to give as much permanence as possible. The bridge thus built stood for a while, but in the great wind storm in the summer of two years ago it was carried away."[23]

The report appears to anticipate, and refute, the argument that the second bridge was "flimsy" or poorly constructed, but eventually draws the fatal conclusion:

"Engineers were sent to work, again upon examination of the bottom. They found that the first reports had been erroneous, and that it was not a solid rock bottom, but was penetrable by piles. The first engineers must have been careless in their work; it certainly was not thorough. They might have struck a series of boulders, and in consequence come [sic] to the conclusion that the bottom was all rock. The engineers' second report, showing the bottom to be partially soft, decided the department to try another description of bridge; the crib-work plan was abandoned, and piles were driven into the bottom. At the narrows piles of at least fifty feet are needed. It is difficult to drive a pile of that length satisfactorily in a hard bottom. They did not penetrate the earth more than five feet. Then they were braced firmly together by heavy supports, placed diagonally. It was suggested to the engineers that to make the piles secure it would be wise to place great granite boulders at intervals of say every twenty feet, and anchor the piles to these by heavy chains. Orders, it is stated, were given to have the piles thus secured. Mr. Connor, of Moncton, was given the contract to do the work, and the task of replacing the bridge was pushed rapidly to completion. How flimsy the structure was is shown by its collapse, for it has come down in less than two years with hardly a breath of wind moving."[24]

In truth – and in defence of contractor Connors – the forces that were at work on the bridge could be neither seen, nor felt by men on the surface, and the contractor was working on an entirely new kind of project, one with which few engineers in Canada had any experience. The *Herald* commented briefly on the unintended consequences of the plan:

"The tide must have floated it off quietly, but none the less surely. If, as appears was the case, the piles were inadequately secured to the bottom, the tide, if higher than usual, simply made the buoyancy of the bridge too great for it to remain in position, and it was loosened from its hold to the earth and was borne away on the surface of the water. The passing to and fro of trains had a tendency to gradually loosen the piles, and after the lapse of less than two years the final destructive forces appeared which proved fatal to the weakened structure."[25]

Again, there was no reference to any curse, although the stationmaster at Halifax left no doubt there was an air of mystery to the event:

"Station Master R. McDonald was called upon by the *Herald* last evening. Mr. McDonald could assign no reason for the collapse of the Narrows Bridge. He said that at 2 o'clock Sunday morning some people near Richmond heard a crash, which excited no alarm. It sounded something like coal being dumped from a cart. They thought no more about the noise till 4 o'clock this morning when it was seen the bridge was gone. It must have disappeared about 2 o'clock because the tide was not at its highest, which would be about 3.30. …Mr. McDonald could give no theory as to the cause of the disaster. It is a mystery to him, he said. That the bridge had stood the storms and gales, and the nice pressure of winter, yet go down on a calm night, with no unusually high tide, was very strange indeed."[26]

Again, no thoughts of a curse appear to have accompanied the collapse, at least as far as outside observers were concerned. The Moncton *Transcript* simply reported in its July 24th 1893 edition:

"At 2 o'clock Sunday morning the Intercolonial bridge across the Narrows to Dartmouth collapsed. No one knows why, except that it was weak or badly built. It fell in darkness and none knew that it was down till daylight came, when the basin and harbour were seen strewn with wreckage of the bridge. About 2 o'clock, people near Richmond heard a crashing sound, but could not tell what it was till morning revealed the disaster to the bridge. At 8:30 Saturday night the Dartmouth train crossed the bridge and seemed to be all right. There was no wind and the tide was not at its highest when the bridge fell. Its collapse is a mystery. The long section gone extends from the draw near the Dartmouth side to within two hundred yards of the Halifax shore. In September 1891, the same section was carried away by a severe windstorm. It was repaired by Connor of Moncton, and since January 1892, has been in use. The bridge is built on piles 50 feet long, which was driven 5 feet into the bottom and braced together. As originally concluded the piles rested on crib piers to which they were bolted. It looks as though a stone and iron bridge will have to be built if it is to be made safe."[27]

Certainly the *Transcript*, an opponent of the government of the time, saw no native curse at play, but in its July 26th edition, accused Ottawa of being at the root of the problem:

"When a bridge is carried away by a freshet in any part of New Brunswick, the Saint John *Sun* and Moncton *Times* are deeply impressed with the need of an immediate change in the local government. But an Intercolonial Railway bridge between Halifax and Dartmouth falls down merely because it cannot stand up; there is no unusual tide, no undue pressure of wind, even the last train passed over hours before, and yet our contemporaries have overlooked the duty of editorially demanding an immediate resignation of the Dominion government! It however, merely needs the oversight to be mentioned, to cause our two contemporaries with that strict impartiality so characteristic of their usual course, to prove their consistency. The matter is a serious one, and the wonder is that the bridge did not fall when the train was passing over and scores of lives lost. What is the I.C.R. bridge inspector doing that such a death trap should be permitted to exist? Are there any other specimens of similar bridge inspection on the Intercolonial [?]. The road has hitherto borne an excellent reputation for freedom from accidents and it would be lamentable should that reputation be marred. The Minister of Railways owes it to the public to hold a rigid investigation into the absence of a condemnatory report on the bridge, because no one will believe that the department would have permitted the use of a bridge so dangerous in its [condition] as was undoubtedly the Dartmouth bridge, if its condition had been reported."[28]

An inspection was certainly warranted. As the Halifax *Chronicle* noted in its July 24th edition, the event was not entirely a surprise, and the consequences could have extended well beyond the bridge alone.

The *Acadian Recorder* of Halifax weighed in with its own observation on the cause of the second collapse, suggesting that worms had consumed the better part of the piles between the high and low water marks.[29] While this may seem an obvious conclusion for those with experience in maritime construction to draw, it seems unlikely that worms would do in two years what they could not achieve in the seven years that the old bridge was standing.

Despite the prevalence of opinion that the second bridge had been poorly constructed, there is a rational engineering explanation for its demise. The failure may be explained by the analysis of a similar collapse of the railway bridge over the Long Sault Rapids of the St. Lawrence River at Cornwall, Ontario, by the *Scientific American* in its October 1st 1898 edition:

"It is probable that the failure of the pier was due to the nature of the bottom on which it was built. In the first place, the method of building up a heavy pier upon the natural bed of the river is not to be commended, especially when, as in this case, the bottom consists of loose bowlders [sic] overlying a hardpan; for when a bulky object like a crib is opposed to the flow of such a swift river as the St. Lawrence, there is an appreciable increase in the swiftness of the current, and a powerful eddying and scouring action is set up around the base of the pier, which is liable to cut away the bed of the river. Where the foundations are carried down well below the river bed, scouring does not necessarily imperil the stability of the pier; but when, as in this case, stability depends upon the river bottom remaining undisturbed, any scouring and undermining at once threaten to overturn the structure.

There is no question that if undermining is proved to be the cause of the disaster, it will shake the confidence of engineers in this system of foundation. Although, on account of the swift current, it would have been a more difficult and costly undertaking to use the pneumatic process, a more satisfactory foundation could have been secured, as the crib might have been carried down through the overlying material to a bearing on a firmer substance below, where its base would have been protected from the scour of the river."[30]

In the case of the Narrows Bridge, it seems likely the rise and fall of the tides through such a narrow strait imitated the scour of a river current, and similarly washed away the soft mud beneath the crib work.

The rational explanation for the curse may be that it was a natural product of the enmity that existed between Dartmouth and Halifax as a result of the competition for a railway, and was developed to prevent Dartmouth from enjoying the advantages of a railway that became Halifax's after the Nova Scotia Railway began in 1854. Perhaps it had been invented specifically to prevent the construction of a third link across the harbour. One clue to this lies in the rather European portent attached to the number three (three shall rise, three shall fall) which has always been regarded as an ominous sign. Dartmouth had actually been the preferred terminus of Major William Robinson, who conducted the survey for what became the Intercolonial Railway. He noted in his 1848 report to the legislatures of Canada, New Brunswick and Nova Scotia, and the government in England:

"The city of Halifax is situated on the western side of the harbour, whilst the best site for the terminus is on the opposite shore at Dartmouth.

The distance to Quebec from the latter will be four miles shorter than from the former; and one great advantage is, that its shore line is as yet comparatively free from wharves and commercial establishments, and an extensive terminus can be formed there at less expense and inconvenience than on the Halifax side, where the Government Dockyard and private establishments would interfere materially in the selection of a good site for it.

At Dartmouth it is expected that vessels entering the harbour will be able to unload at the railway premises, or probably into the railway cars, whilst an equally good terminus is to be had at Port Levi, opposite to Quebec. The same railway cars, loaded from the ships in harbour at Halifax, will thus, after running an uninterrupted course for 635 miles, be delivered of their contents into the boats if not the holds of vessels in the St. Lawrence. The same can of course be done from the River St. Lawrence to the vessels waiting in Halifax harbour.

Such an uninterrupted length of railway, with such facilities as its termini, will be, it is believed, unequalled in the world."[31]

This recommendation did not sit well with the wealthy and more politically influential merchants of Halifax, who were unwilling to risk having their commercial interests play second fiddle to the city that Dartmouth would have become, had the railway terminated there. It was for this reason that the Halifax lobby readily agreed to ante up the £100,000 levy placed on property in the city in order to help finance the creation of the Nova Scotia Railway. It is a matter in need of further investigation whether or not the levy was actually paid, but such a prerequisite for a railway put the Dartmouth merchants out of contention. Joseph Howe – who was the driving force behind the construction of the Nova Scotia Railway from Halifax to Truro, the first leg of what would become the federally owned Intercolonial Railway – was among those who saw Halifax as the more suitable terminal for the line.

The effort to bring a railway line into Dartmouth without the necessity of crossing the harbour had actually begun some years before the Narrows Bridge collapsed. In his as-yet unpublished *Legislative History of Nova Scotia Railways*, John Cameron notes:

"Legislation was needed to encourage some shorter extensions. The then Town of Dartmouth was authorized to pay a subsidy of $4,000 a year for up to twenty years to any company building a line from Windsor Station (or any other point on the Intercolonial) to Dartmouth (*Consolidated Statutes of Nova Scotia 1882, c.37*). This was a large sum, as the statutory limit on the total tax levy for Dartmouth was only $15,000 at the time. Any funding from the Government of Canada would be used to reduce the cost of the subsidy to the Town. The authority was replaced the next year and also allowed the Town to strike a deal with the Government of Canada to extend the Intercolonial, and gave the Town the option of paying the subsidy at the rate of $2,000 per year for forty years. The Central Short Line Railway Company (Consolidated Statutes of Nova Scotia, 1892, c.131) was eventually chartered to construct this line (notable incorporators included Fletcher Wade, of the Nova Scotia Central and Simon H. Holmes) but, in fact, the Government of Canada through the Intercolonial actually built the connection."[32]

Even as the Intercolonial construction was underway from Truro to Moncton, Dartmouth residents were still lobbying for their town as its terminus. The Halifax *Morning Chronicle* of December 15th 1871 reported: "We understand that the Literary Society in connection with the Dartmouth Y.M.C.A. intend to discuss this evening the question of the relative merits of Halifax and Dartmouth as a terminus for the Intercolonial Railway."[33] The prize was of inestimable value, after all, Robinson had predicted (in somewhat contradictory fashion) in his 1848 report: "One of the undoubted results of the railway will be to make Halifax, if it be made, as it ought to be, the Atlantic terminus, the great emporium of trade for the British Provinces and the far west."[34]

So who would have created the curse, if not the burghers of Halifax, anxious to see their city become that emporium? The possibility exists that the curse was an invention of the Mi'kmaq to prevent the railway from further encroaching on their community. They would have seen how the Nova Scotia Railway had split the "African community" (as Howe knew it, later known as Africville) in what is now Fairview, and the Narrows bridge continued that interruption by bringing the railway across the harbour from Richmond to Norris Cove, and through the Mi'kmaq village at Tufts Cove. (The Tufts Cove Mi'kmaq settlement was destroyed in the December 6th 1917 explosion resulting from the collision of two ships in Halifax Harbour.) In addition, there is evidence to suggest that while the indigenous people had a friendly relationship with Joseph Howe, their relationship with the Nova Scotia Railway, and later the Intercolonial, was not as cordial.

When the passenger trains began arriving in Halifax, the Mi'kmaq had found a new market in which to sell their baskets, berries and trinkets – at the station, to throngs of tourists. This offered a daily market to the native craftsmen, in addition to the Friday and Saturday markets held in the city at the time. This seemed to be a healthy enough symbiosis for both the natives and the railway, but it changed in 1864, when Jonathan McCully became commissioner of the Nova Scotia Railway. In his attempt to increase the profitability to the line, everything that had previously existed as a free market became subject to franchising and licensing – everything from newspapers to sandwiches, liquor to baskets and berries became subject to bidding for the right to sell on or near the railway platforms. At the same time, while railways in Maine allowed the natives to travel for free (usually as "blind baggage" – that is, by riding on the platforms on the outside ends of the coaches) the Nova Scotia Railway and its federal successor insisted on charging full fare. By 1867, there was evidence that the railway management's attitude toward the indigenous members of the community had strayed far from the tolerance shown by Howe. The Halifax *Morning Chronicle* in its December 29th 1867 edition lamented this:

"A few months ago a poor Indian was crushed to death at the Richmond Depot. The cause of his death was the insufficiency of a barrier placed across the rails to prevent the cars running back too far. The servant in charge had seen the cars several times jump over this, and from pure negligence failed to report the case. At the end of the rails was a building against which the cars bumped when they overran the sleeper placed across to stop them. Standing against the building one day was the Indian referred to. The cars were shunted in with too great force, and caught between the foremost one and the building, the Indian was crushed to death. His Lordship the Chief Justice, in an able charge to the Grand Jury, regretted that the inefficient state of the present railway law prevented the bringing of an indictment against the parties through whose culpable neglect the accident had happened. The man was killed by the carelessness of the servant or servants of the Railway Department, and that Department was liable for the acts of the servants in the damage sustained. And, judging by the heavy sums Railway Companies are compelled to pay in case where limbs are broken in England, if the like case had happened there the widow and orphans would have recovered a just compensation for the damage they had sustained in the loss of their bread winner.

The other day the father of the unfortunate man, with a petition setting forth the destitution of the widow and orphans, waited upon Avard Longley, Esquire, Chairman of the Railway Department, soliciting alms. And this was the written reply:

'The Railway Department, provided $100 are raised, $20.

(Signed) Avard Longley'

Now, we ask what right has the Railway Commissioner to put any such condition upon his gift demanding from the public that they first shall pay five times as much as the Department, whose servant or servants, by gross carelessness, were the occasion of the poor widow seeking relief.

A laudable economy in the disposition of the public funds is certainly desirable, but such small-souled charity is worthy the execration of the community."[35]

If the aim of the native community had been to invent a curse to discourage rebuilding the bridge, and thereby remove the railway from their community, it failed, as Lawson's history has shown. The branch line that later made the connection between Dartmouth and the main line at Windsor Junction continued on from the point where the bridge had made land (near what is now the site of the Bedford Institute of Oceanography.)

Invention or not, belief in the curse was strong enough to oblige the municipal bridge commission to take extraordinary measures to prevent a similar fate from befalling the third bridge over the waters of Halifax Harbour in 1955. As with the Tremaine and Starr plans, some time elapsed before any action was taken to create the "stone and iron" structure called for in the July 24th 1893 of the Moncton *Transcript*. The Tibbetts history in the *Herald* notes:

"Discussion on constructing a durable bridge didn't resurface until 1928 when the Halifax-Dartmouth Bridge Company was formed in response to Dartmouth merchants' complaints about the cost of shipping goods by rail from Halifax to Dartmouth.

Plans for a bond issue to raise $3 million for construction were ready to proceed in 1930. But politicians delayed those plans due to the Depression. The Second World War further disrupted plans."[36]

The Angus L. Macdonald bridge, named after the premier of the day, would carry a curse of its own making, in that the financing was conducted with the use of Swiss currency, which over the years – and because of international money markets and inflation – added millions of dollars to the structure's debt. This aspect was far from the minds of the men who formed the bridge commission. They invited the Grand Chief of the Mi'kmaq nation of the time to perform a ritual to remove the curse at the opening ceremony on April 2nd 1955, in the hope of allaying the fears of the motorists who were to use the bridge. As Martin notes:

"Libby Meuse, an elder from Indian Brook First Nation, Shubenacadie attended the ceremony when the curse was removed. She was born in 1928, so she would have been 27 years old. She offered the following information:

'I remember attending the ceremony where they removed the curse from the bridge. My mother and father were invited to attend. My father was Martin Sack, my uncle Joe Sack also went with them. They had to wear Indian clothes and my mother and father went into the long building afterwards for the feast or dinner. Old William Paul, Dowie Howe we called him, Chief Joe Julian from Millbrook, Chief Ben Christmas and his daughter Mary from Membertou, and Jim Paul from Indian Brook were there. Jim Paul was the youngest and they told him to perform the dance while they sang hymns and prayed in Mi'kmaq, in our tribal way. It was the respectable way to show people this is an honour to be asked to do this. They sang and prayed while Jim Paul danced up to the middle of the bridge and back'."[37]

What Martin, and other popular historians of the curse fail to note, however, is that the shaman who performed the ceremony had his own doubts about the validity of the threat. James Paul was quoted in the April 4th 1955 edition of the *Chronicle-Herald* :

"A full-blood Micmac [sic] Indian, garbed in a heavily-beaded but featherless costume of long ago, brought a 'good wish' to the opening ceremonies of the Angus L. Macdonald Bridge Saturday, and did his best to scalp a myth that an Indian curse hovered atop the towers of the gigantic structure.

Chief James Paul, who described himself as an unofficial representative of his tribe, but a sort of 'chief of good wish,' told reporters that he had never heard of any curse on the bridge in any tribal pow wow.

'I do not believe there is any curse on this bridge,' he said earnestly."[38]

The tenor of the reporting was indicative of the attitude toward native people at the time, language that would never be used in today's media, and it may be indicative of a point that will be made later:

"James Paul, now a resident of Waverley, reminded that that the previous bridges were flimsy, just about as flimsy as the legend.

'I have never heard any curse discussed at any Indian council,' he said. 'Indian people are in peace with the white man. We have no cause to argue at all'."[39]

The story includes a portion of the popular poem, and acknowledged that not everyone subscribed to the curse: "Most sceptics contend the poem was produced by someone in the current century, and the entire legend is nothing more than a myth."[40] But in making the concession, the reporter immediately seizes upon the "evidence" of the collapsed railway bridges to validate the legend. The report is at least helpful in that it provides a name for the brave who is alleged to have cast the fateful incantation on any form of harbour crossing: "He said that he had never heard of a curse on the bridge, despite the stories of Chief Oeurehavo who, legend has it, cast a spell on 'links across the water'."[41]

The cavalier use of native imagery, evident in the lead of the *Herald* story, is not without precedent in Atlantic Canada. For years until about the mid 1980s, amateur weather prognosticators based their forecasts on the wisdom of the "old Indian," an unnamed native who could predict events like severe winters with deep snow if hornets' nests were observed high in the trees that summer. This same "old Indian" was credited with developing phrases like "big flakes, little snow; little flakes, big snow" – an adage which practical observation holds to be generally true – but when pressed, no one could provide a name for the sage. It may be that, as with the "old Indian," the Halifax bridge curse is more indicative of an attitude by Canadians of European origin toward the Mi'kmaq population, than it is a veritable aspect of Nova Scotia railway lore.

Some of the more ardent adherents of the power of curse believe the third phase, the threat of death, was reached when Macdonald died in 1954, a year before the bridge bearing his name opened, but this was not enough to satisfy some people. For some, the fact that five construction workers met violent deaths on the site of the bridge in that same year did more than fulfill the ominous prediction of the curse.

Sceptics pointed out, however, that the bridge was not built across the Narrows; the supposed site of the original curse and the section now spanned by the A. Murray McKay bridge, built in 1970. After all, none of the Halifax Harbour ferries that had routinely crossed the water between the two cities since 1752 ever succumbed to catastrophe... but the routes of those vessels never took them close to the Narrows.

Only recently has the threat of the curse on shipping in the harbour been invoked in connection with the terrible explosion that devastated Halifax December 6th 1917, when a French munitions ship collided with a Belgian relief ship at the Narrows. The resulting blast killed more than 1,500 people, and was the largest man-made explosion prior to the atomic bombs dropped on Japan in 1945. Laura MacDonald's book *Curse of the Narrows: The Halifax Explosion, 1917* (Harper Collins, 2005) chronicles the events of the day, and the immediate aftermath, and the title may have been inspired by the stories she heard as a girl growing up in the city.

There is a third explanation for the existence of the belief in a curse on the Halifax bridges. It may have been invented by the city media. This would not be without precedent. One of the most popular "curses" in modern history – that of George Herman "Babe" Ruth on the Boston Red Sox baseball team – was propagated by newspapers to explain the team's abject and often spectacular failure to win the World Series since 1918. Legend holds that Ruth, who was a popular player on the team from 1914 to 1919, cursed owner Harry Frazee – or perhaps it was Fenway Park, the team's home – for selling his contract to the New York Yankees in order to raise money to finance Frazee's production of the musical *No, No, Nanette*. The Red Sox had won three World

Series with Ruth as a pitcher prior to the sale. They did not win again until 2004. The Yankees went on to have one of the most storied dynasties in professional sports.

It was not until 1986, however, when the Red Sox appeared on the verge of winning the Series against the New York Mets, that the notion of a curse first became popular, when *New York Times* sportswriter George Vecsey wrote an article listing the errors that accompanied the collapse of the team in Game Six. When the Mets won Game Seven, Vecsey wrote an article headlined *Babe Ruth's Curse Strikes Again*. It may have been that the idea was first planted by United Press International (UPI) sports writer Frederick Waterman, who noted in a story previewing the American Leage championship of that same year that when the Sox traded Babe Ruth to the Yankees, "he carried away with him the good luck and winning touch of the Red Sox." From that point onward, the media made the curse both a popular and convenient way to explain the team's failures.

A newspaper is the most likely source of the hoax of the Halifax hex, with the railway bridge collapses providing sufficient factual basis to lend credibility to the invention.

The curse does not appear in popular usage until the advent of the opening of the Macdonald Bridge, and it does not appear to have been known when Nova Scotia Museum director Harry Piers began gathering his information[42], leading to the conclusion that it was developed some time between 1928 – when taxpayers were faced with the proposition of financing a $3,000,000 bridge – and 1955 when the bridge opened. What may be difficult to determine is whether this "legend" was spread with deliberate editorial mischief in mind, or by well-intended but misguided trust in a flawed or faulty source.

Another clue leading to the conclusion that the curse may have been the creation of a newspaper lies in the poem cited by Martin and the 1955 *Chronicle-Herald* reporter, a portion of which is quoted at the opening of this work. The poem in its entirety is in the collection of the Nova Scotia Archives and Records Management Service, as a typewritten rhyme apparently penned for the Halifax *Evening Mail*. It is unattributed and undated:

> Legend of the Narrows' Bridge at Halifax
> (For the Evening *Mail* – December 12)
> We were smoking our pipes on a glorious night
> Outside the camp, 'neath the moon's clear light.
> Tired, but happy and stretched at our ease,
> With nothing or none but ourselves to please.
> "Can you tell us a tale?" I asked our guide,
> of forest or mountain or land and tide?
> And I looked at his honest and rugged face
> With scarcely a vestige of time's rude trace.
> "Did you ever hear the legend?" he said,
> "of the Narrows' Bridge," - and I shook my head.
> "I can tell you that, for I know it well."
> "Then come along – your story tell."
> "Long, long ago when those woods were wild
> and their sweet rich fragrance was undefiled,
> An Indian brave built his wigwam there

And his squaw was with him, so young and fair,
He loved her well, this Indian bold,
But her love for him was weak and cold.
She had given her heart to a pale face man
Outside her tribe, not of her clan –
And she pined for her lover until one night,
When the moon-beams were filling the woods with light,
He came to her wigwam and spoke so low
That none could hear, and he begged her go
Just down the beach where the wavelets play,
But her Indian brave was not far away.
He watched them meet with a loving kiss,
Not a single word did his keen ears miss
He saw her step in her lover's boat
And over the moon-lit waters float.
He followed them, in his swift canoe,
When she saw him coming, ah – then she knew
But a sudden cloud o'er the moon was thrown
And the night winds echoed a dreary moan.
He gained their boat on the side he stept,
And his guilty squaw to her lover crept
He drew his hatchet, - the blow fell wide
Instead of the lover he struck his bride.
She staggered and fell, no cry she gave,
But sank to sleep 'neath the restless wave.
The coward pale face was seen no more,
His boat went quickly to the other shore.
The Indian stood in his light canoe,
And his hatchet under the waves he threw,
Then raised his hand to the Heavens above
And this is the legend – of hate and love –
"Three times a bridge o'er these waves shall rise,
Built by the pale face, so strong and wise.
Three times shall fall like a dying breath,
In storm, in silence, and last in death."
And now, young sirs, you know the tale
Of the Narrows' Bridge – once in storm and gale,
It fell with a crash, and then again
In silence it fell, neither storm nor rain,
In death, says the legend, the bridge shall fall
No matter how solid they build the wall.
The Indian's legend will sure come true, -
And, now young sirs, a good night to you."[43]

(One tell-tale erroneous detail, however, is that the second railway bridge did not fall "in silence" as the curse predicted, but with an audible crash, as described by stationmaster MacDonald.)

The *Evening Mail* was combined with the *Chronicle*, *Star* and *Herald* in 1949 (to become the *Chronicle-Herald* and *Mail Star* newspapers), perhaps providing a further clue to era in which the legend of the "curse" was born. If the newspaper did invent the legend of the curse, it may have done so without any malicious or mischievous intent. Indeed, the newspaper may itself have been duped into believing the story, perhaps by a writer whose sole intent was to sell Halifax as a tourist destination.

Tourist travelogues were a very popular, and profitable genre of literature at the time that the first Narrows bridge was being built, and reputable writers like Charles G.D. Roberts (1860-1943) were making a good living writing for railways like the Dominion Atlantic Railway, which sold its "*Land of Evangeline*" image to Americans visiting Nova Scotia eager to relive the Longfellow experience (although Longfellow never visited the province.) What better way to attract Americans to Halifax, than to lure them with the story of a curse placed on the harbour bridge as the result of a romantic tragedy? (Roberts mentions the railway bridge across the Narrows in his landmark work, *The Canadian Guide Book* – published in 1891 by D. Appleton of New York – but makes no reference to any curse. He makes no reference it in his second work, *The Land of Evangeline and Gateways Thither*, published by the Dominion Atlantic Railway in 1895.)

The *Evening Mail* poem may have played a part in this plot, for it could well have been styled upon the example of Wilfred Campbell's (1858-1918) *Legend of the Restless River.*

The two poems have common elements; a body of water cursed by an Indian, and the waters become inexplicably violent as a result of the incantation. Campbell's poem –which is set on Lake Huron – reads in part:

"It was a curse and worse,
A curse on the Restless River;
Moons and moons ago,
Before the ages of snow,
And ice and rains that shiver,
Came the curse of the restless river.

What was this terrible curse?
Never in tale or verse,
Did singer or chief rehearse;
Warrior sang it never;
But only the Manitou,
Who knoweth all things, knew
The moons and ages through,
The secret of Restless River.

Where other streams might sleep,
In eddies cool and deep,
Beneath where cascades leap
In sunny snowy surges;

With never a dreaming place,
With never a breathing space,
In one wild tortuous race,
Its maddened tide it urges."[44]

The poem concludes:

"And the dreamy Indian girl,
As she sees it waters curl,
In many a silver whirl,
Hath pity on Restless River,
For she knows that long ago,
Its tides that once were slow,
By reason of some dread woe,
Went suddenly swift forever;
That a dread and unknown curse,
Was laid on the Restless River."[45]

Campbell was known as one of Canada's "Confederation Poets," a closely-knit group to which Roberts also belonged, and sought to promote Canada's great lakes region as a place where the nation's leaders could: "…spend a week or a month every summer somewhere on the shores of the…great lakes, away from the jar and jangle, the vulgar jostle of the crowded money-marts…"[46]

Of course, there always remains the possibility that the curse does exist. As Carroll has noted, they are difficult to prove, and thus can be equally difficult to disprove … unless a third bridge is built. There are those who suggest a third bridge is still waiting to collapse, perhaps a third railway span across the harbour, which is considered every time the new "super city" of Halifax-Dartmouth is obliged to consider the financial and environmental ramifications of its overcrowded transportation infrastructure. Interurban commuter light rail service – perhaps a modern-day version of Halifax's old tramway – has been strongly advocated for Halifax and Bedford, around the shores of the cursed waters, but few seem willing to tempt fate by suggesting a line be built directly across the harbour to Dartmouth, by way of the narrowest point, which may still be under an ancient curse.

CHAPTER 3

The White Horse of Merigomish

"Dreams are not comparable to the spontaneous sounds made by a musical instrument struck rather by some external force than by the hand of a performer; they are not meaningless, not absurd, they do not imply that one portion of our stockpile of ideas sleeps while another begins to awaken. They are a completely valid psychological phenomenon...." [1]
- Sigmund Freud, *The Interpretation of Dreams*

THE premonitions of disaster, referred to by Freeman Hubbard in the first chapter, can run the full spectrum of emotions — from a simple lingering unease, to terrifying and lurid dreams that paralyze the victim with fear. Such dreams are often simply described as being the result of bad food, alcohol, over-medication, or a deep-seated weariness in the hard-worked individual. Some just cannot be explained away. It took seven decades for Freeman Prevoe's dream to come to the public's attention, and the two deaths that resulted were all but ignored at the time, a period when death claimed the highest born of the land as easily as the simple working man.

Queen Victoria ruled for sixty-four years over one of the greatest empires that history has ever known. Her death on January 22nd 1901 cast a pall over all her subjects; most of them had never known any other head of state, and most had spent the last thirty-five years of her reign devoted to her. In the weeks following her death every newspaper ran stories of fond remembrances of her, and hopes for the success of the reign of the new king, and of continued prosperity for the empire. This reverie was broken only momentarily in the Halifax *Herald* of January 26th with the terse report of an accident that did not follow the standard coverage of such incidents, even though they had become frequent events on the Intercolonial Railway:

"A terrible accident happened on the I.C.R. near Merigomish at midnight. A special freight from Mulgrave to Stellarton, in charge of Conductor Joe Mahoney, Engineer Wheaton, Moncton, and Fireman J.W. Blackwell [sic], Stellarton, encountered a wash-out. The engineer was instantly killed. The fireman was terribly scalded, and his head crushed in. He was taken to hospital and after suffering intense agony died at daylight. Blackwood was in the great collision at Stellarton a year ago, when seven persons were killed. He was standing in front of the workingman's car, jumped and had his jaw broken. Both men were single.

Only half an hour before the accident another special train passed over the track where the washout occurred.

The cars were all piled up. All trains have been transferred. One of the brakemen had just returned to the van from the engine when the accident occurred.

The washout was 60 feet long and 20 to 25 feet deep. In the pocket of Wheaton was found $145. His watch was running but badly damaged. The entire train of eight

Above: The White Horse Wreck. Dreams as precursors of terrible events are commonplace in the lore of North American railways. The damage to the train was total, and devastating, as this 1901 photo of the salvage crew bears witness.
(Donald Robeson collection)

cars excepting the van ran into the washout. Coroner Kennedy held an inquest with the following result:

'That the said W.R. Wheaton …his death by being crushed in the wreck of the train of which he was diving, said wreck being caused by a washout on the I.C.R. The jury would exonerate the railway officials of all blame in the matter.'

Wreck is said to be, excepting the collision, one of the worst in the history of the I.C.R.

Only a week ago another incident occurred not many miles from the same, then caused by ice on the rails and a train of 12 cars went off the track."[2]

The local newspaper, New Glasgow's *Eastern Chronicle*, carried nothing of these events; its pages were crammed with lengthy dissertations on the royal family and the history of Victoria's reign. Only the letter of an anguished father in its February 14th edition — copied from the Moncton *Transcript* — served to notify Pictou County readers that a terrible tragedy had occurred closer to home:

" I beg to call the attention of the public through your columns to the death of my son, William B. Wheaton, who was killed on the 24th day of January, ult., while acting as engineer on the train between Stellarton and Port Mulgrave. A washout occurred on this part of the line by which a piece of the roadbed, about 60 feet long and 20 to 25 feet deep was washed away, and the engine plunged into this hole, causing the immediate death of my son and inflicting fatal injuries upon the fireman, who died a few hours afterwards. From the information I have received, the death of my son and the fireman are the result of improper management of the railway in not having the road properly patrolled by section men."[3]

Daniel Wheaton, of Upper Sackville, New Brunswick, claimed that had any amount of "reasonable diligence" been observed, the washout would have been detected, and the life of his son could have been saved. He wondered aloud why the time and place of the coroner's inquest was withheld from the public, and raised the question of whether a cover-up was underway to absolve railway officials from any implication in his son's death.

As if to reinforce the senior Wheaton's claim about the dangers of the job, the newspaper carried another brief report immediately below his impassioned letter:

"A bad smash up occurred to the fast express from Halifax to Sydney, on Tuesday evening at 5.30 in the I.C.R. yard here. The engine, tender and three cars were thrown from the track, but happily no persons were injured. What occasioned the accident is a matter of conjecture. Some suppose that when the air brakes were put on, the train running at a good rate of speed, caused the tender to be thrown from the track at the frog, at the upper end of the freight shed. Others suppose that there was a defect in the frog, and still others say a broken wheel occasioned the accident. The train was in charge of Conductor Dan McIntosh. Lewis Sterrat, of Truro, engineer. A large number of men were employed from the time of the accident in clearing away the track. Everything was cleared away by noon yesterday."[4]

And so it was that a tragedy on the Intercolonial might have otherwise been consigned by history to the chapters of the merely "ordinary" events of the era. Before investigating the claims of Daniel Wheaton about the responsibility for his son's death, however, a witness close to the Merigomish events has painted an eerie picture (the area of the wreck is known today as Egerton.) Richard Griffin Jefferson was a substitute driver on the Intercolonial in January of 1901. A native Nova Scotian (he was born at Round Hill, Annapolis County in 1867), and an experienced engineer on other parts of the system, his trip from Stellarton to Mulgrave on January 25th was his first on the section that is still known today as the "Rollercoaster." His story did not come before the public until published in the New Glasgow *Evening News* of February 2nd 1972:

"At the roundhouse, I found a little Rhode Island eight-wheeler, taken over with the Halifax and Cape Breton in 1884. She could haul about ten loaded cars of that day. Murdock McLeod was my fireman — and Murdock, too, I was meeting for the first time.

Ben Wood was Conductor and volunteered to ride on the engine as Pilot. Fred Fraser was head brakeman, and Hiram Dewar was rear brakeman.

Our orders leaving Stellarton were to run to Avondale regardless of Flemming's signal — that is, the signal carried by the last train west. Stand Rules were still 12 years in the future, and we were running under the Intercolonial dispatching system.

After some hours shunting at New Glasgow, we left the old Nova Scotia Railway main line behind and headed out for Mulgrave over the dark and dismal trackage of the Eastern Extension."[5]

Jefferson noted the track between Stellarton and Mulgrave had been a focal point of controversy for more than forty years, and had been controlled by the federal government for the past eighteen years. In that tine, traffic had proved to be only "normal" until the development of the Sydney steel mills, when traffic and tonnage grew exponentially.

"…At the time I speak of there was not a switch light to be seen in the 79 miles between New Glasgow and Pirate Harbour, and on a night such as this we navigated "by guess and by God," as the sailors say, with the aid of an occasional glimpse of some familiar landmarks close to the track.

The ties were rotten and the rails were small."[6]

This last remark will help reveal the real villain sought by Daniel Wheaton seventy years before Jefferson brought it to light, but it was unnoticed — or ignored — by the government of the time. He called the line a series of "hogbacks" that saw many of the engines ill-suited to such terrain running freely through the hollows and downhill, but straining to reach the summits.

With no switch lamps in place at the sidings, it was often possible to run through open switches, which were difficult, if not impossible to see on the night he made his run. With so many of the crews drafted from other divisions, and unfamiliar with the road, a recipe for disaster had been created:

"Just this side of West Merigomish (now Egerton) the engine gave a heavy lurch and the train seemed to drag a little more, but she righted herself, and we plowed along through the storm to Avondale, 24 miles out. There we got orders to meet Joe Mahoney's westbound freight special at Marshy Hope, and after six miles toil up the hill, we pulled in the sidetrack and waited until the dim oil headlight of 91 — a brand new, Moncton-built Mogul — shone through the night.[7]

Engineer W.R. (Bill) Wheaton, a close friend who had come down from Moncton a few months before me, had heard that I was on the road for the first time that night, and slowed down and stood in the gangway with his torch lighted and exchanged greetings. As they pulled by, I noticed that there were only two men in the cab and wondered where the brakeman might be, but gave it no thought until later.

Their taillight faded around the curve, and that was the last train Bill Wheaton ever met.

We backed out of the siding to get a run for the hill.

It was still a terrible night."

At this point Jefferson's details of the events go well beyond Coroner Kennedy's brief assessment, and the terse statistical count carried in the Dominion of Canada

Above: This photo taken in 2000 shows the stretch of track at the highway overpass at Egerton, which is believed to be the site of the White Horse wreck.
(Andrew Underwood)

Sessional Papers of 1902, where the minister of railways gave his reports of accidents that had occurred the previous year. Some of these details seem to have come from the coroner's account, but others must have been swapped amid the chat at the roundhouse at Stellarton:

"I remember as I passed Brierly Brook seeing an engine and 13 cars almost submerged. The conductor said they had jumped the track several days before, and until the water went down it would be impossible to clear the wreck. At Antigonish, the red order board was on, and after giving the fireman a hand to shake down the fire and oil the engine, I walked back down to the telegraph office to see what they had for us.

The warm, cozy office, with its mellow lights and red-hot potbellied coal stove offered a striking contrast to the cold, stormy scene outside. There were several railroaders talking with the operator, but as I entered the Morse key suddenly began to chatter, and he held up a hand for silence.

'Listen! FR calling RA! That's strange. Something wrong!' he said. 'There's no night operator at Merigomish!'

The same thought must have struck the dispatcher at New Glasgow at the same moment, for he answered immediately and said:

'GA. Go ahead FR.'

Then our operator read aloud to us, word for word, the message that went over the wire.

On the previous night, Mahoney's special had left Stellarton eastbound for Pirate Harbour with Bill Wheaton engineer, James W. Blackwood fireman and Freeman Prevoe forward brakeman. There was another brakeman — the rear man — but I forget his name."[8]

James Blackwood was something of a celebrity on the subdivision, because of his close brush with death just a little over a year before. On September 28th 1898, he had been a passenger on a crowded workmen's train which had collided head-on in 'Adams Cut,' between Stellarton and Westville, with an excursion train from the Short Line, loaded down with passengers for the Halifax exhibition. Both engine crews and three passengers died instantly in the crash – a total of six fatalities and twenty-four injuries, the second worst in the history of the Intercolonial at the time.

Blackwood was standing in an extremely dangerous position on the open platform of the first car, right next to the engine, but was thrown clear with only a broken jaw. He had been listed as a passenger in the official report, not a railway employee.

Prevoe was also new to the road, described by Jefferson as being "a quiet, serious chap who had been educated by the monks at Tracadie…He was kind and honest and a good brakeman, but a great believer in signs and portents and, among those who knew him well, was thought to have a gift of 'the second sight."

Prevoe had told some friends about a vivid, recurrent dream he had been having, of a handsome white horse. In his dream he was aboard a train, at the same place each time the horse would suddenly appear and pace the locomotive for short distances. The horse would then climb the embankment and run ahead of the train, and Prevoe would awaken. Fearing ridicule from his colleagues, Prevoe made no mention of his premonition to them.

"Out on the road he kept a sharp lookout for the apparition, if such it was, but saw nothing — until January 23.

Then, just as they reached the place indicated in his dreams, the phantom suddenly appeared, easily pacing the engine for a hundred yards. Prevoe sat rooted for a second, then leaped across the cab shouting to Wheaton to stop before they ran down the animal now galloping down the center of the track ahead of them.

At the first alarm Wheaton's practiced hand closed on the Engineer's air valve, but he could see nothing on the track — and neither could Blackwood. The brakeman insisted the horse was still there and begged them to put the brake on. Another second and it was gone from Prevoe too."[9]

In Jefferson's account, Prevoe told his colleagues of his dream, and suffered their torments all the way to Pirate Harbour (Mulgrave), quietly assured that he had experienced a premonition of death. The eastbound trip passed without further incident.

On the return trip, on reaching Antigonish, Prevoe removed himself from the cab of the locomotive and went to the caboose, on the pretence of eating his lunch. He stayed in the caboose all the way to the tank at Piedmont in Pictou County, despite being urged by his conductor to return to the cab.

Jefferson claims that after passing Piedmont, the conductor realized Prevoe was missing, but supposed that he was riding up ahead. Nearing West Merigonish, Mahoney thought he saw a faint light under the centre door, opened it and discovered Prevoe with his lighted lantern standing just inside the dark van looking out the front door at the rocking freight car ahead. Asked why he had not gone forward at Piedmont, Prevoe said he felt in his bones that something was going to happen, but added that he would go to the engine over the tops of the swaying cars.[10]

He got no further than the door that would get him to the ladder and on top the boxcars for the trek to the head of the train, when a series of crashes and jolts threw both men to the floor. Getting to their feet they looked out into the darkness and found the front of the caboose hanging over a raging torrent of black water and scalding steam.

It was the freshet that Jefferson's train had experienced on its eastward trip, the last train to cross that section of track, and into which Wheaton had unknowingly driven his locomotive, to be killed instantly. There was, ironically a horse involved. Conductor Mahoney had gone to a nearby barn, commandeered a horse, ridden four miles through the storm to Merigomish Station and told the operator to call New Glasgow for help.[11]

As if to further validate Prevoe's premonition, the accident had occurred at midnight, the same hours as foretold in the fireman's dream. Freeman Prevoe is an enigma in his own right, for his name does not appear in either 1901 or 1911 census...but the name of eight-year-old Carrie Prevoe appears in the 1911 census in New Glasgow. This young lady would become Dr. Carrie Best, a champion of human rights and member of the Order of Canada.

Her father, James Edward Prevoe, was listed in the 1911 census as a labourer in the town coalmines (the Allan Shaft), as was his son, John Henry. James Edward Prevoe was born in Merigomish. He was listed in the 1901 census as James E. Provo, of African descent and a labourer in the iron works. They were Baptists in their faith.

There were no Provoes listed in the 1901 census, and of the male Provos in 1901, none was listed as being a railway worker. No one bearing the Provo surname in 1911 was recorded as being a railway employee.

The census enumeration was done on April 26th, almost three months after the accident, so perhaps one of these men went by the nickname of "Freeman," and had changed his employment in the aftermath of the terrible wreck.

In his investigation of the wreck, published in the Canadian Railroad Historical Association's *Canadian Rail* of December 1981, Tony Mackenzie also quotes retired telegrapher Donald MacLeod's version of the events, but Mackenzie opens with a statement that one bearing such a Scottish name should surely have doubted:

"Ghosts and railroading do not seem to mix. Dispatchers and roadmasters have no time for such things. Seemingly the very nature of the business — heavy machinery, haste, noise, bright lights — should leave no room for the supernatural."[12]

As far as Nova Scotia is concerned — and the Piedmont valley in particular — ghosts are the staple of local lore, and those of Celtic extraction ignore them at their peril. In Celtic tradition, the white horse is powerful image, since it was the steed of the goddess Epona (also known by the Welsh as Rhiannon, and the Irish as Macha), worshipped for her powers of energy and fertility. Those of Celtic extraction were often encouraged to offer a prayer to Epona for a safe journey, for the spirit was a patron saint — of sorts — for the traveller.

This facet may have been lost upon Prevoe, whose monastic/Baptist education would have made him far more aware of the white horse images contained in the Bible's books of *Revelations* and *Zechariah*. In both books, the imagery is of a horse associated with judgment and death. The vision in *Zecahariah* 6, describes four chariots led by horses of different colors from between two mountains of bronze to patrol the earth and appease God's wrath. The first chariot is drawn by red horses, the second by black horses, the third by white horses, and the fourth by dappled horses. In *Revelations* the horses are associated with the four Horsemen of the Apocalypse, and Prevoe's fear may have been spawned by the prophesy of *Revelations* 6:8:

"And I looked, and behold a pale horse: and his name that sat on him was Death, and Hell followed with him. And power was given unto them over the fourth part of the earth, to kill with sword, and with hunger, and with death, and with the beasts of the earth."[13]

Be that as it may, there were some less-than supernatural forces at work behind the Merigomish wreck, and Daniel Wheaton was not entirely correct in his assertion that the railway officials were at fault. Indeed, the Intercolonial's managers had long recognized the need to upgrade the track between Mulgrave and Stellarton, especially with the increased traffic the line faced from the newly created steel mills of Sydney.

Commenting upon the tabling of the Laurier government's supplementary spending estimates — some $7,244,135 worth — the Toronto *Globe* commented in its June 27th 1900 edition:

"With respect to railways it is proposed to expend a considerable sum upon the Intercolonial Railway. The business of the line, as is well known, has increased at such a tremendous rate that further and more improved equipment is necessary, as well as more modern facilities at certain points of the route, and notably at the Straits of Canso, where $250,000 is to be spent upon a first-class ferry service. Then, too, there has been such a wonderful industrial expansion at Sydney, Cape Breton, and a consequent startling increase of traffic, that the portion of the line in that district calls for better and heavier steel rails. All this means the expenditure of money, but it must be remembered that there will be a correspondingly large increase in the earning power of the railway in consequence of these improvements, and the revenues will show a satisfactory addition on the right side of the account."[14]

Of the total amount, the government had earmarked $420,000 for steel rails and fastenings, $80,000 towards strengthening iron bridges, $12,000 for improving telegraph service. By January of 1901, as the Moncton *Daily Transcript* reported in its January 15th edition, that amount had increased significantly when Railways Minister Andrew G. Blair announced that $2,000,000 would be spent on improving the Intercolonial between Truro and Sydney. The facilities at Mulgrave were inadequate, as only a single car could be transferred at once. The government ordered a 2,000 horsepower steel scow from the Armstrong Whitworth Company, costing $250,000, which would carry four cars each trip. On Port Hastings side a wharf was to be built a mile and a half south of Mulgrave, doing away with the switchback.[15]

Railways minister Andrew Blair steadfastly proclaimed his commitment to making the line safer, as he told the Montreal Gazette, duly reported in the *Transcript*:

"The development of the coal and coal resources of Cape Breton," said the Minister, "in my opinion is a one of the greatest questions the Dominion has ever been called up on to grapple with. It is bound to open up limitless possibilities — not only the Maritime Provinces but to the whole Dominion. The contiguous existence of both iron and coal in immense quantities has been for centuries one of the principal reasons for England's national greatness. We have similar conditions in Cape Breton.

The possibilities of the remote future we can speculate about, but the prospects of the immediate future are so apparent that I have felt it my duty as Minister of Railways to

Above: Francis Hector Clergue. The failure of the American would-be steel tycoon to fulfil his contract on the Eastern Extension Railway between New Glasgow and Mulgrave led to the conditions that caused the wreck at Merigomish in 1901.
(Courtesy Sault Ste. Marie Public Library Archives)

prepare for an enormously increased business over the line of the Government Railway from the centre of these new industries at Sydney to your own city, the commercial metropolis of the country. This necessity I saw some years ago when I obtained from parliament a large vote of public money, which is now being used in relaying the line between the junction at Truro and Sydney with heavy eighty pound rails."[16]

Seeking to deflect some of the criticism directed at him, Blair retreated to a familiar stand for federal cabinet ministers, blaming any delays in taking action on the deliberation in the House of Commons.[17]

While all spending this sounded like affirmative action, where the government and its railway failed was in its choice of contractors to replace those "small" rails referred to by Jefferson. One man caused the delay. Francis Hector Clergue failed to carry out his contract with the Intercolonial to deliver 25,000 tons of steel rails. Blair had purchased the rails in England from the Channell Steel Rail Company, at Clergue's request, and on his account.[18]

F. H. Clergue (1856-1939) earned his place in Canadian history for his success as the creator of the Algoma Central Railway and Algoma Steel Inc., the surviving remnants of his empire, but the American-born entrepreneur was also infamous for his colossal failures, more often than not based upon reckless and wild judgment than unfortunate economic circumstances. Indeed, the former lawyer's flamboyant promotional tactics were inevitably followed up by poor execution.

This is illustrated in the city of Sault Ste. Marie's on-line history, which notes that his most dramatic failure came in 1888 when he announced that he had been given a contract to build a railway across Persia (now Iran). With $25,000 of financing secured in England, Clergue traveled to Persia where he formed three separate companies: the Persian Railway and Construction Company, the Persian Electric Light Company and the City of Tehran Water Works. Each of these companies had a capitalization of $1,000,000.

Clergue had not kept up-to-date with the relations between Persia and Russia before entering into negotiations with the Shah of Persia. Soon after he began the survey work associated with each of these three companies, the Russian government intervened and secured for itself the first right of refusal with respect to the construction of all railroads in Persia for a period of forty years. Clergue was frozen out of the construction project, losing the money provided by his backers in the process.[19]

With his two brothers, Clergue had arrived in Sault Ste. Marie in 1900 intending to establish a fantastic empire based upon electrical power production and steel milling, but it fell apart magnificently in 1903, and the report of his inability to fulfill the contract to supply the new rail to the Stellarton-Mulgrave portion of the Intercolonial was a harbinger of that fall from industrial grace. He almost immediately left the country to pursue other opportunities in Russia, returning to Canada in 1910.

By that time, William Wheaton and James Blackwood's deaths were mere unhappy memories, and Freeman Prevoe may still have been holding tightly to the secret of his awful dream.

CHAPTER 4

The Grey Lady of Inverness County

"I dwell with a strangely aching heart
In that vanished abode there far apart
On that disused and forgotten road
That has no dust-bath now for the toad.
Night comes; the black bats tumble and dart;" [1]
- Robert Frost, "Ghost House"

POPULAR mythology – especially that created relatively recently by Hollywood – has developed the idea that ghosts are creatures of terror. Within the lore of the paranormal, however, there are myriad ghost stories about women, dozens of them involving an apparition known as a "Grey Lady," which is neither evil nor malevolent.

England has more than its fair share of these ladies: Denbigh Castle in Wales is haunted by a Grey Lady, and while the castle is better known to be haunted by a boy who peers from its windows, nothing is known about the Grey Lady. Many people who live near to the castle, and several visitors, all claim to have seen her.[2] The Grey Lady known as Margaret Neville has been seen wandering around one of the towers at Warkworth, Northumberland, and a ghost of a young man has also been spotted running along the castle walls. A trip to the cellars will produce the feeling of an uncanny presence in the room, which could be the result of the wine cellar's previous use as an overflow prison.[3]

The Georgian Theatre Royal of the City of York is said to be haunted by a Grey Lady, a nun who fell in love with a young nobleman, and upon their secret being discovered, she was thrown into a windowless room which was immediately bricked up to form the poor woman's living prison…and tomb.[4] At Beamish Hall in County Durham, legend has it that the Grey Lady there was in love with a Mr. Shafto, but was promised to another by her father. On her wedding day she ran to Beamish Hall to escape her soon-to-be husband and hid in a casket in the lowest cellars within the hall. Unknowingly she locked herself in and suffocated to death.[5] Perhaps the most famous Grey Lady is that which haunts Glamis castle, the former home of Queen Elizabeth, the Queen Mother. Centuries before, the young and beautiful Lady Glamis was accused by King James V of being a witch and was burned at the stake.[6]

In the United States, there is a Grey Lady of the Civil War era at the once all-female Columbia College, in Boone County, Missouri, an area of intense conflict during the rebellion. It is said one young student was engaged to a Confederate soldier and vowed to wear only grey clothing so long as her lover wore his grey uniform. He was killed not far from the school, and she jumped from the three-storey Conservatory building, now known as Williams Hall.[7] In all these cases the recurrent theme appears to be one of unfinished business. Recounting the story of a similar apparition at a mill in the

Above: This quiet road leading to a secluded cove near Judique is where Dr. Michael and Ethel Ojoleck experienced the Grey Lady. The former railway right-of-way crosses from left to right. This photo was taken in 2005
(Simon Underwood)

north of England, in his book *The history of the supernatural in all ages and nations, and in all churches, Christian and pagan: demonstrating a universal faith*, William Howitt makes note of the reason for that ghost's existence:

"Mr. Proctor adds that a lady, a clairvoyant, a stranger to the neighbourhood, being thrown into the clairvoyant state, and being asked to go to this mill, described the priest, and the grey lady; and added that the priest refused to allow the female ghost to confess a deadly crime committed in that spot many years ago, and that it was the troubling cause of the poor woman."[8]

The Grey Lady is usually glimpsed as a fleeting figure clad in grey, passing almost imperceptibly through buildings and creating an indescribable presence. Helen Creighton in *Bluenose Ghosts* describes several Grey Lady sightings in this province, the most notable at Stony Beach in Annapolis County, but only one in Cape Breton, at Marion Bridge.[9] So the Grey Lady of Inverness County, on the western shore of Cape Breton Island, presents a particularly challenging tale to prove or disprove. Her occurrence – perhaps one of her last – is described by Judique resident Ethel Ojoleck, wife of local dentist Dr. Michael Ojoleck, both of whom experienced the phantom one evening during a walk to the nearby shore.

"We were expecting our first child, and we were naturally nervous, worrying about the baby's health, our readiness to become parents, our finances, all those normal worries young couples have," she said. "We were walking down the trail that led across the old railroad tracks, and at once both of us were struck by a sense that we were not alone, although no-one could be seen nearby."[10]

Ethel Ojoleck said she heard a voice telling her not to worry, that their future would not be fraught with the misfortunes they were conjuring up for themselves. A great sense of inner peace swept over her. Describing the experience to neighbours some time later, the Ojolecks were amazed that there was neither surprise nor alarm shown toward the news of the apparition. "They told us how it was that she haunted the place, and how some people had actually seen her at various times," Dr. Ojoleck said.[11]

This reaction was apparently predictable, as Janette MacDonald has indicated, noting ghost stories have been told and such phantoms have been experienced by certain individuals as long as Judique has been a community: "Even though the science and materialism of the twentieth century was supposed to have killed such beliefs as these. Perhaps the most familiar ghost stories concern the return of people who have left debts unpaid upon leaving the earth. Stories have been related stating how they returned and spoke to some persons asking them to pay off the debts for them. After the debt was paid, they were seen or heard no more."[12]

As with many other ghostly tales, however, any investigation into the Judique phenomenon is hampered somewhat by a lack of corroborative documentation. There is no mention of the Grey Lady phantom in J.L. MacDougall's *History of Inverness County* or *The Inverness and Richmond Railway*, by Allister William Donald MacBean. This is not because either work lacks any emphasis on local colour. MacDougall's history devotes a large section to the famous fighters of Judique, who had been inducted into folk lore in Moses Foster Sweetser's *The Maritime provinces: a handbook for travelers* (J.R. Osgood, Boston, 1875).[13]

MacBean's work commemorates the route of the *Judique Flyer* the quaint mixed train that ran between Port Hawkesbury and Inverness for so many years, and has now become immortal in fiddle player Buddy McMaster's tune of the same name. Historian Colin Churcher of Ottawa has offered the most concise account of the little railway:

"The Inverness Railway Company was incorporated in 1874. The name was changed to the Inverness Coal Field and Railway Company in 1875 and to the Inverness Coal, Iron and Railway Company in 1886. The Inverness and Richmond Railway Company was incorporated in 1887 to construct a railway from the district of Margaree to Mabou, and Port Hood, and Port Hawkesbury, with a branch to Whycocomagh. A line was built from Inverness Junction on the ICR to the town of Inverness, 60.5 miles, and opened for traffic on June 15, 1901."[14]

The operations of the railway and the coal mines were inseparable, and soon became a target for Western Canadian railway magnates William McKenzie and Donald Mann, who were developing the Canadian Northern as a competitor to the Canadian Pacific Railway and had plans to incorporate smaller lines like the Inverness & Richmond Railway, and the Halifax & Southwestern on the Nova Scotia mainland, into a transcontinental network. Canadian Northern fell into financial difficulties shortly after the end of the First World War, and McKenzie and Mann were obliged to transfer it to the federally owned railway system, becoming incorporated into Canadian National in 1922. Churcher notes:

"The line was leased to CN [Canadian National] from Feb, 1 1924 until purchase in 1929. It was declared a work for the general advantage of Canada in June 1929. Canadian National operated the line until the late 1980's, when the line's biggest customer, the Evan's Coal Mine, was shut down due to flooding."[15]

The line closed in 1986. In spite of its extensively documented history there is some reason to doubt that the Grey Lady has any tangible link to the railway. Judique resident Virginia MacIsaac knows of the legend, but the version with which she is familiar has the woman following carts along local roads, behind the rear wheels, and MacIsaac has heard of only one incident when anyone attempted to communicate with the phantom in order to try and identify her.[16]

These discrepancies are not necessarily fatal to the veracity of the legend, for there are some elements common to other ghost sightings. One version of the story is that this Grey Lady is the wife of a railway employee, and she waits alongside the tracks for her husband to return from a trip during which he died in an accident.[17] At first glance, the story of a wreck at Glendyer (the community was also known as Glen Dhu, or Alexander Station), some forty-three kilometers (26.8 miles) north of Judique appears to hold clues to solving the mystery experienced by the Ojolecks. MacBean makes note of the fatal accident that occurred in 1912, but the Sydney *Record-Post* of July 11th 1912 offers more detail:

"Another train disaster has followed in quick succession to the one to the *Maritime Express* yesterday. On the Inverness Railway this morning a special passenger train running from Inverness jumped the track just before reaching Glendyer station.

The engine, carrying four cars along with it, was precipitated down the embankment. Assistance was called from Glendyer, and a gang of men at once set to work to clear the wreckage.

The body of the engine driver, William Campbell, was found crushed beneath the weight of his engine. He was dragged out and found to be suffering agonies through bodily injuries and scalds from the escaping steam of the locomotive.

Dr. Kennedy, of Mabou, was called and he reached the scene of the wreck speedily, but it was found that Campbell's injuries were beyond medical aid, and he died an hour after the accident. He was a native of Troy, Port Hastings, but had lived for some time past in Port Hastings. He leaves a widow and one child. Campbell was a first class railway man. He had a host of friends and sincere sympathy is expressed with his widow in her terrible loss."[18]

The passengers escaped any injury, the car at the rear of the train remained upright and on the rails. The wreck occurred within hours of another tragedy, the derailment of the *Maritime Express* at Grand Lake near Halifax, which took the life of three men; and a matter of days after a serious wreck at Alba, Cape Breton. All three accidents were caused by sun kinks, the bending of steel rail by the intolerable heat of the sun.

William J. Campbell was 31 years old at the time of his death (and a resident of Inverness, not Port Hastings, as the Sydney *Record* claimed), and is buried in the

Above: The wreck at Glendyer, July 11ᵗʰ 1912. The widow of locomotive No. 79 engineer William Campbell was obliged to walk past this site on her way to his funeral.
(A.B. MacMillan photo, Jay Underwood collection)

old section of the Newton Road cemetery at Port Hastings, with his sister Catherine (who died in Boston in 1889 at the age of 25), and his father Allan Campbell, who died 1892. He left behind his wife, Mary Florence (née MacNeil), and their three-year-old daughter Mary, also known as Mae.[19] The Halifax *Herald* of July 12ᵗʰ 1912 made note of a sad irony surrounding William Campbell's death, which occurred in the worst accident in the history of the road at the time: "… A feature of this tragedy is that [he] was relieving the regular engineer this morning, making the trip for today only."[20]

Campbell's grieving widow raises the possibility that she could be the Grey Lady, but what makes this story more compelling is the time frame in which the accident occurred, less than three months after the sinking of the Titanic, the White Star Line's "unsinkable" passenger liner that went down 323 nautical miles off the southeast coast of Newfoundland on its maiden voyage April 14-15ᵗʰ 1912. Many of the bodies of the 1,503 victims of the sinking were recovered and delivered to the dock at Halifax. Dozens of the victims were buried in two Halifax cemeteries. The event shook both the world and the faith that had been growing in the invulnerability of technology of the era and that had its epicenter in Nova Scotia. The impact of the Titanic sinking has been examined in sociologist Kai Erickson's book, *A New Species of Trouble* (1994). In her review of that book, Mary deYoung of the American Academy of Experts in Traumatic Stress notes:

"In April 1912, the luxury liner Titanic struck an iceberg on its maiden voyage and sunk in the north Atlantic, killing 1500 of its passengers and crew, and challenging the western world's belief in God and its faith in technology."[21]

The name of William Campbell also appears on the memorial at Belfast city hall in Northern Ireland. He was a passenger aboard Titanic, and had been an apprentice joiner at the Harland & Wolff shipyard where the ship was built. The excitement of the Titanic disaster was especially pervasive on Cape Breton Island; the distress calls from the stricken ship were picked up at the cable station at Hazel Hill, across the Strait of Canso in Guysborough County. Regionally, there were several reports that the ship had been seen off the coast of Prince Edward Island!

If, as some researchers believe, ghost legends grow as the result of a collective social trauma, the Glendyer incident could well have fuelled the legend of the Inverness Grey Lady. What serves to disqualify both Florence Campbell, and the Titanic tragedy as factors in this story, however, is the fact that Florence Campbell remarried in 1932 (to another railway man, John (Jack) Hugh Skinner, a conductor on the Sydney & Louisburg Railway) and died in Halifax in June of 1984. She is buried in the United Church cemetery at Inverness.[22] Among those unwilling to believe there is a connection between Florence Campbell and the ghost is a grandson, John Wilson, son of Mae Campbell:

"I know nothing about the Grey Lady...nor am I aware that such a story might have anything to do with my grandmother. There was never anything mentioned in the household about such a connection during the long life of my grandmother. She lived with my parents from 1956-1984 and she died in my parents' home. The only story that I remember her telling concerns her traveling from Inverness to Port Hastings where my grandfather's funeral was being held. The track at Glendyer had not been cleared, so she had to get off one train, walk around the site of the accident and board another train for Port Hastings."[23]

Wilson concedes that the tragedy could have been a catalyst for such a story:

" I realize that many stories about particular ghosts tend to be tied to historical figures, that is, that the ghost is seen to be the ghost of an actual real person. So it is certainly possible that someone thought the Grey Lady might be tied to my grandmother, but usually ghosts appear only after the person is dead and my grandmother made it to the age of ninety-eight, some seventy-two years after my grandfather's death."[24]

Had Florence Campbell been the Grey Lady, her appearance could then only have occurred in the last twenty-two years, and other versions of the story have the spectre following people as they made their way in carts along the local roads. This suggests some antiquity can be attached to the story, but there is no way to determine when the ghost first made its appearance.[25]

There were several other fatalities on the line, including a series recorded by MacBean, where five men died between August of 1904 and January of 1907:

- Allan McIntyre died July 31st 1904 in the yard at Inverness when he was jammed between two coaches during a shunting session. He ran between the coaches after having given the engineer the signal to "Go Ahead"[26]

- On November 15th 1904, Frank P. Gordon was killed at Long Shore Beach after the engine of his train from Port Hastings to Glencoe overturned, crushing him between the cab and the boiler. According to the November 18th 1904 edition of the *NovaScotian*, Gordon, a 24-year-old single man from River Phillip, near Oxford Nova Scotia, was the lone fatality as the result of a severe gale that lashed Nova Scotia that day. The train on which he was conductor left Port Hastings at 4 a.m. that day and ran into a washout. His engineer was not seriously injured.[27]

- February 11th 1905, fireman Allan MacLean was killed at Port Hawkesbury as he alighted from a moving locomotive and fell under the engine.[28]

- Brakeman D.A. J. MacIsaac died at Port Hastings, November 8th 1905 when his head was caught between two coaches as he was uncoupling the train.[29]

- Brakeman Angus Proctor died at Inverness January 7th 1907 when he was run over during the uncoupling of cars.[30]

Below: The Ghost Beach bridge, near New Town, Cape Breton in 2005. Staff of the Canadian military engineering school at CFB Gagetown, New Brunswick, installed the bridge on the new section of the Trans-Canada Trail in a single day in May of 2003. The bridge is close to the site of the 1925 wreck that resulted in the death of eight-year-old Martin Carr.
(Andrew Underwood)

Any one of these men could have left a grieving wife or mother to haunt the tracks on which they regularly ran.

Another version, suggested by someone who prefers not to be identified with the story, indicates the woman was a passenger who died aboard a train. This has proven to be difficult to verify from newspaper records, and may simply be a reflection of the popularity of stories of "phantom travelers":

"Phantom travellers are ghosts of humans and animals which haunt travel routes, stations, and vehicles, and are universal in folklore and legend. Some appear real while other hauntings involve only sounds, lights, sensations, and smells.

In one case, a man, Colonel Ewart, secured a compartment by himself on the train from Carlisle to London. He dozed off but later awoke feeling stiff and strange, and noticed that a woman in black was sitting opposite him. A black veil obscured her face, and she seemed to be looking at something on her lap, though nothing was visible. Ewart spoke to her but she did not respond. She began to rock back and forth and sing a soft lullaby, though there was no child with her. Suddenly the train screeched and crashed into something. Ewart was knocked unconscious by a flying suitcase. When he came to, he left the train and learned that the accident was not serious. He then remembered the woman in black and returned to the compartment, but she was nowhere to be found. Ewart was told that no one had entered his compartment after him.

Months later, a railway official told Ewart that the woman was a ghost who haunted the line. According to legend, she and her bridegroom had been travelling on the train when he stuck his head too far out the window and was decapitated by a wire. The headless body fell into the young woman's lap. When the train arrived in London, she was found sitting in the compartment, holding the corpse and singing a lullaby to it. She never regained her sanity and died several months later."[31]

Such lore may have been a possible source for a ghost story on other stretches of the province's railways, where accidents were common, but in fact, the newspaper record shows that passengers on the Inverness line fared better than most; there appears to have been only one passenger fatality on the line.

This raises a third and potentially more plausible origin – again related by a source seeking anonymity; that the Grey Lady is the mother of a child killed on the tracks. There is some promising historical validity to this version of the story, for the Moncton *Daily Times* of April 8th 1925 records a tragedy that occurred to a young boy on the line:

"One fatality has occurred as the result of a derailment of the C.N.R. passenger train on the Inverness branch in Nova Scotia at a point near Port Hastings on Friday morning last, when Martin Carr, a boy of eight years died at his home in Port Hawkesbury, Monday, following injuries received in the mishap.

While no details have been received at C.N.R. headquarters here as to the cause of the accident, reports coming from Port Hawkesbury are to the effect that two cars of the train jumped the rails and turned over an embankment and that other passengers in the cars were injured, among whom were two ladies whose injuries are reported to be serious, some members of the train crew also received a bad shaking up.

The condition of the road bed on that branch in certain sections is reported to be very rough following the recent thaws and it is probable that spreading rails was responsible for the run-off."[32]

The scene was close to that of the 1904 accident that killed Frank Gordon, but the significance of this wreck was made more apparent by the Halifax *Morning Chronicle*, which noted in its April 4th 1925 edition: "Today's run-off was the first accident of anything like a serious nature that has occurred on the branch since its operation was undertaken by the C.N.R. a year ago."[33]

The notion of the boy's grieving mother being the Grey Lady gains some validity when one considers the report of the Halifax *Morning Chronicle* of April 7th 1925:

"NEW GLASGOW, April 6 -- Word was received here this morning from Antigonish that Martin Carr, aged eight, of Port Hawkesbury, died in St. Martha's Hospital on Sunday from injuries in the wreck of the express on the Inverness line.

The little chap was taken to the hospital on Friday afternoon, following the accident, which derailed three cars of the express train at Long Beach, near Port Hastings on Friday morning. The deceased was suffering from internal injuries, and it was found necessary to operate. It was discovered that a broken rib had pierced the liver. The boy died shortly after the operation, As far as can be learned here, the boy was an orphan and was living with his uncle, Daniel McIsaac, in Port Hawkesbury."[34]

There may be, however, some risks involved in relying too heavily on contemporary newspaper reports. According to his death certificate, Martin Buckley Carr was only five years old when he died, but the certificate does not record the year of his birth. His parents' wedding date confirms the boy would have been no more than five when he died.[35] These discrepancies in the record combine to offer an attractive suggestion that this child's mother could be the Grey Lady of Judique. The facts refute this.

Martin Buckley Carr's parents were Leonard Carr of Guysborough, and Mary A. Graham of Inverness. Leonard Carr was the son of Abner Carr of East St. Francis Harbour, Guysborough County, and Margaret Diggins. He married Mary Ann Graham, daughter of John Graham and Catherine Gillis, at St. Andrew's parish church in Judique, on August 13, 1918.[36] Martin was not an only child. The family relocated to Gloucester MA. and the other children included Lillian and Kezia (Kaye) Carr, and a second son, Martin Jr. He was also not predeceased by his parents, at least not by his mother, who died July 16th 1981.[37]

Those more willing to believe in such things might make the point that Mary Graham Carr is the perfect candidate to be the Grey Lady, searching the line for her son; a line that was taken over by the federal government with the expectation that service would be safer than it had been under Mackenzie and Mann's superintendence. It is typical of the nature of a Grey Lady – mourning the loss of her only child – to offer comfort to Ethel Ojoleck as she anticipated the birth of a new member of her family, while the two shared a moment by the abandoned tracks near their homes.

That so many versions of the story of the Grey Lady exist is not surprising, given the tradition of the area. This has been noticed by "outsiders" like Kristin Nord, of Western Connecticut State University in Danbury, Connecticut:

Above: Long Beach bridge, near the Canso Causeway, as it appeared in the mid-1900s. (Photo courtesy Gut of Canso Museum)

"To the south along the coast are the predominantly Scots Catholic settlements of Judique, Port Hood, Mabou and Inverness. These are inhabited by hearty descendants of the Scots Highlanders who arrived from the early 1800s on. This is where you'll hear "the Gaelic" in the music and in the cadences of English as it is spoken.

The island's settlers clung to the oral traditions they brought with them – and Cape Breton, even today, like a migratory route studded with pins, is a place showcased in its music and its stories – some dating back to the Middle Ages, a legacy from pre-industrial Europe; others pure Nova Scotian, connecting the people with the province's natural environment and history. A visitor quickly grasps that this oral tradition serves as a tribal language of sorts, imparting the culture's landmarks and re-enforcing common values."[38]

There are other examples of the tradition. Virginia MacIsaac of Judique recalls a further intriguing story from the immediate region, the appearance of ghostly lights and sounds along the line of the railway.[39] Mary L. Fraser, who noted the Inverness County events, has also documented these phenomena:

"Years before a railway was built through Inverness Co., trains were seen and heard. One evening, a man who lived a mile above Mabou River, when returning from feeding his cattle in the barn, heard the sound of a train passing where no one ever thought it would pass. He called his wife and children, and they all listened to the clatter of the "Judique Flier" [sic] as it made its way over the grassy slopes and wooded hills of this beautiful countryside. Contrary to all expectations, when the railway was built several years later, the route it took was through that particular part of the country."[40]

Such stories have existed for as long as the railways themselves, most commonly in North America, and especially in the United States. One of the most persistent accounts comes from Maco, North Carolina, where a story of strange lights dates back to 1867 and involves a railroad man named Joe Baldwin. The Atlantic Coast Line Railroad had just been rebuilt and now included a small station once called Farmer's Turnout (now Maco.) Baldwin was a conductor for the Atlantic line and his job involved riding in the last car of the train. One night, as the train was steaming along, he realized that his car seemed to be inexplicably slowing down. With one look, he realized that it had become uncoupled, and there was another train following behind! He was sure that train would crash into his slowly moving car.

Baldwin ran out onto the rear platform of his car, wildly waving his signal lantern, trying to get the attention of the engineer of the train behind him. The engineer paid no heed, crashing into the car where Baldwin had remained at his post. Baldwin's head was severed from his body.

A witness to the accident reported that just seconds before the trains collided, Baldwin's lantern was hurled away, hitting the ground, finally coming to rest in a perfectly upright position. Shortly after the accident, the Maco light was seen along the tracks, and has been appearing ever since, becoming a popular curiosity on warm summer nights. "Cars can be parked along the highway and the curious can walk the hundred or so yards down an old road to the train tracks. Rarely is anyone disappointed… because the light is one of the most regular anomalies in the south."[41]

Canadian railways have similar legends, such as that at St. Louis, Saskatchewan, northeast of Saskatoon. This story contains elements similar to that of Maco (italics added for emphasis):

"The ghost train has been a part of St. Louis for as long as anyone can remember. When the rail line was abandoned and the tracks removed years ago, some thought the phenomenon would end. It didn't. Locals say the ghostly apparition can still be seen almost every night.

Whatever it is, its enduring nature is fertile ground for imaginative legends and theories. One of the most persistent of these involves a *hapless conductor who was struck down and decapitated by a train while doing a routine check of the tracks.* It's said the bright, yellowish light belongs to the old steam locomotive pulling his train. The smaller, red one, is *the lantern he's using in a futile search for his head.*"[42]

The story of the Mabou lights and sounds may also be explained in the context of the forerunners recorded by Fraser.

Perhaps it is just an eerie coincidence, but the route of the railway from Port Hastings to Judique took the train over the 33-metre bridge at what today is known as Ghost Beach, near Troy. The three kilometer-long beach is traversed by the old railway line as part of the Trans-Canada hiking trail and – as MacBean notes – was once called Long Beach, site of the 1904 wreck that killed Frank Gordon, and the 1925 fatality that took Martin Carr's life.

CHAPTER 5

The Whiteside Terror

From ghoulies and ghosties
And long-leggedy beasties
And things that go bump in the night,
Good Lord, deliver us!

- Traditional Scottish prayer

MANY people are reticent to relate their ghostly encounters for fear of ridicule, or facing accusations of not being entirely in a sober state of mind at the time. Certainly there have been stories of such incidents where alcohol has been involved, but what of those where some of the witnesses were stone cold sober? As has been noted previously, railways were particularly sensitive to the use of alcohol by their employees, to the point where the very suspicion of its use was grounds for punishment ranging from "reduction in rank" to outright dismissal.

The federally owned railway, the Intercolonial (later Canadian National), had led the way in this respect with the edict issued April 5th 1885, but smaller railways were quick to follow the lead, including the Cape Breton Railway, which connected with the Intercolonial at Point Tupper on the Strait of Canso, and ran to St. Peter's with ambitions of one day becoming the southern island route to Sydney.

The uncompleted line was to run from Louisbourg to New Brunswick, with a branch to Halifax by way of a massive bridge spanning the Strait of Canso. It was intended to make Louisbourg's harbour the leading port for all trans-Atlantic shipments, being at least two days closer to English ports than Halifax. The entire project was part of what was at one time called the European and North American Railway. When funding for the project began in 1884, it was immediately in competition with the Dominion government, which also had plans to extend its railway, to Sydney. Construction on the southern Cape Breton line didn't start until 1901, however, and by then the Intercolonial had already reached Sydney Harbour, having monopolized the massive amount of traffic generated by the island's new coal and steel industries.

The first, and only, segment of the southern line – thirty miles from Port Hawkesbury to St. Peter's – was completed in 1903, but by that time the promoters were obliged to accept that traffic levels would not justify the high cost of completing the remaining sections. Extension of the line was abandoned. In 1920 the right-of-way was sold to the Canadian government and, along with the Intercolonial, the Cape Breton Railway became part of Canadian National. Despite its small stature, as historian J. William Calder has noted, the Cape Breton Railway Company followed the federal standard religiously, including rule 'G' of the 120-page code of conduct issued for the federal lines: "The use of intoxicants by employees while on duty is prohibited. Their use or frequenting of places where they are sold is sufficient cause for dismissal."[1]

One might expect employees returning to duty after a "night on the town" to offer stories of unusual occurrences, and dismiss them as the usual product of their bacchanalia, but how easily can those same occurrences be dismissed if sober employees witnessed the same events…more than once? Cape Breton Railway section hand Stephen Patrick Sampson put down his experience on paper, and although some details have been lost to time, they can be corroborated to the point that the story cannot be ignored:

" One summer the Cape Breton Railroad Company decided to fence their railroad property from St. Peters to Point Tupper so they sent a man and his son, and an old man for company, from George's River with a work car to live in while they were getting the job done. The work car was put on a siding at White Side. The railroad foreman, Alfred Morrison, ordered a flanger car to be put on the same siding the boss's car was on.

From St. Peters to Sporting Mountain, we walked to our work. The section foreman got lumber and got the boys to build bunks and shelves to store our food and dishes. While the flanger car was in St. Peters, the boss who was doing the job got news from his home that some relative or friend died, so he went back to his home and took his son and the old man with him. After they were gone and the flanger car was moved to the same siding that the boss's car was put on, we started to work during the day.

One night some of the boys went to a dance in Louisdale. They took a pump car that we had and travelled to the dance which was about twelve miles from where our car was, so one of our boys made a dish of fudge and we played cards until eleven o'clock, after which we went to bed."

Sampson makes no secret that his comrades had been indulging in some off-duty drinking, and since they were not returning to report directly to work or under public scrutiny, they were not technically in violation of the company rules, as long as they had sobered up by morning. It didn't take that long!

"Everything was quiet until we heard the boys coming home from the dance, singing. I suppose they had a few drinks of liquor and felt happy. They took the pump car off the main line and put it on the siding. Then this big object appeared before them, so tall they couldn't see the head. The boys froze right where they were, too frightened to speak. They made a dash for the car we were in and when we opened the door they fell face first on the floor. The next day it was the talk of the place.

The third night, one of the hired men, Dan Thibeau, said to all of us: 'There is no such thing as ghosts, I'll prove that to you tonight.' So we left it at that, and waited for our brave man to perform his magic. We all went to bed early because we were tired after our day's work on the fence. Just at twelve o'clock, we all were awakened from the noise on the roof of the car. It sounded like a big stone was rolling from one end of the car to the other. One fellow got up out of bed and lighted all the kerosene lamps. Our magic man picked up a switch broom that was near the bunk we were in. This kind of a broom has a sharp steel point on one end and a broom on the other, used on switches to break ice and sweep it away. He had the broom in his hand and shouted, 'Who ever in hell you are, I dare you to come in this car.'

With that, the bolt that was on the door… started to turn and the door started to open. The two Morrison boys braced their feet on the door trying to keep it shut but their legs buckled. The door opened wide and this big creature all in white clothes floated down to the other door and disappeared.

Our brave boy had the broom in his hand but never tried to use it on the ghost. He turned towards me and said, 'You are going to sleep alone tomorrow night. I'm going to sleep with one of the other boys. I think he is after you.' I felt the cold chills creeping over me. What if it should happen? What would I do? I had to face it."[3]

Sampson notes the car was the scene of yet another ghastly attack the next night, as pots and pans, dishes and food were flung about by and unseen hand. It was during this episode that he recalls feeling the icy grip of a hand around his neck, squeezing it noticeably and forcing a scream from him. He stayed awake for the remainder of the night.

When the section foreman returned from the funeral at George's River, his crew told him of the haunting drawing tears of laughter from the boss's face, and the predictable taunts that they were all crazy. His ridicule was soon replaced by terror, as the crew went to bed only to awoken by someone hammering on the door. One of the men opened the door, to find his boss, in his underwear with a lamp in his hand, pale as a ghost, shivering from fright, and his son behind him: "By God," said the foreman "our car was picked up about thirty feet in the air and dropped down back on the rails. The old man was thrown out or his bunk onto the floor. He is sill unconscious. The rest of us landed on the floor." The crew then jeered their boss with taunts of "You don't believe in ghosts! There is no one here that could lift a box car." The foreman promised his crew that would be the last night anyone slept in that car.[4]

Below: Whiteside railway siding as it is today. Nothing remains of the track from Port Hawkesbury to St. Peter's at this point, although much of the line is being converted into a public hiking trail, perhaps inviting more encounters with the poltergeist.
(Simon Underwood)

Sampson gladly walked fifteen miles the next day, to the home of a friend who had gone to the United States "pogy fishing" (looking for work). It was at this home that he learned of further hauntings after his departure, when an impromptu dance hosted by the crew who had stayed at the site was "crashed" by the phantom, and later again when boys intent upon damaging the now-abandoned boxcar were scared off by the apparition. Sampson soon discovered there was an explanation for the eerie encounters, and that others had experienced similar unsettling events:

"The section foreman told me that the flanger he was using was taken from Harbour Boucher. They used it then behind the plow to clear the railroad yard. The reason it was taken off and put on the Cape Breton line was that a man got killed operating it. The section foreman said the end of the car that the man was killed on was abandoned and the same kind of a rig was put on the opposite end of the car. It seems that the flange was operated by a lever that had two guardrails on both sides to keep it up off the track. There were holes on both sides of the guardrails and a pin was put through to keep the flange up at night. Leaving Point Tupper before or after a snowstorm, he had to operate this flanger. He would get the car turned around because that man's spirit was still on his job. He said he was nervous at first to see him there, but he got used to it!"[5]

What Sampson and his comrades had witnessed is commonly referred to as a poltergeist (from the German, meaning quite literally, "noisy ghost.") These apparitions are frequently associated with violent, or mischievous acts, but they are not necessarily malevolent. The problem with suggesting that a poltergeist may have been involved in this incident lies in the public's perception of Hollywood's depiction of the phenomena as malicious child-snatching ghouls.

But the culture of the poltergeist pre-dates Holywood by more than a century, and has become the focus of serious scientific study at places like the Rhine Research Center Institute for Parapsychology at the University of North Carolina. Although there have been a fair number of bogus events, such frauds have been easily exposed, while events like those at Whiteside have not. There is no record of the Cape Breton incident in the archives of this institution.

The poltergeist is typically manifest by the movement – often violent – of objects about a room, accompanied by inexplicable noises. Despite the Hollywood stigma, for more than seventy years the phenomenon has become the focus of serious scientific study at the Rhine Research Centre. The activity usually occurs around a single person – known as the agent – who is considered to be the one who generates the phenomenon as the manifestation of psychological trauma.[6]

There is also another type of poltergeist, known as the "wrath version," created when someone experiences a strong rage at the time of death. The deceased is supposed then to return from the afterlife to fulfill their vengeance, a will so strong that it cannot be relinquished or forgiven.[7]

In order to determine if the Whiteside poltergeist was a case of localized mass hysteria, or a valid episode of a poltergeist, there have to be some corroborating facts. The difficulty with the corroboration of the story is that Sampson's granddaughter, Leona Hussey – to whom he described the events, no doubt in all sincerity – has no way to determine when it took place. She suspects that it could have been as early as 1913, for her grandfather later left Cape Breton to work in Halifax and survived the Halifax Explosion of December 6th 1917.[8]

Perhaps the most compelling corroboration of Sampson's story comes from the involvement of Alfred Morrison, named by Sampson as the foreman in charge of the work. Cape Breton genealogical researchers Maureen McNeill and Allan Gillis unearthed the following details: Alfred Morrison (1882-1957) was a St. Peter's native, and among the first to be hired on by the Cape Breton Railway. A good Presbyterian, he and wife Matilda (Burns) raised four sons and a daughter. His job obviously paid well, for the 1911 census shows they were able to hire a domestic servant to help Matilda with the household chores.[9]

He and Matilda are buried in the Lakeview Cemetery at St. Peter's (she died in 1968) with an unnamed infant child who died in 1909.[10] Could this event have been the "relative or friend" who had died, to whom Sampson referred in his story? Perhaps he merely mistook the Morrison family tragedy for that of the "boss" of the work. If so, could Morrison's grief have been the agent through which the poltergeist acted? It was Morrison, according to Sampson, who offered the story of the ghost in the flanger car as an explanation for the tumultuous events that had been experienced.

Certainly there were some substantial snowstorms in the same era that could have led to a fatal accident, especially in 1905 and 1907. Of these two years, only 1905 appears to be relevant to the Whiteside story. The Antigonish *Casket* of February 2nd 1905 carried two stories that might corroborate the tale of the origin of the Whiteside poltergeist:

"A freight train, bound west, was badly wrecked just west of the Monastery platform at Tracadie, Ant. [Antigonish County], on last Saturday night. A broken car wheel caused the accident. Sixteen cars left the track and were hurled down an embankment, where they still lie, some of them. Seven of them were coal laden and a few more were loaded with pig iron. J. Fleming of Stellarton, brakeman, was passing from the engine to the van along the top of the train at the time and was thrown some forty feet. The deep snow on the ground no doubt saved his life. Dr. H. MacDonald was conveyed to the scene, and attended the injured man, who appeared to be suffering internally. It is thought, however, his injuries are not serious. The wrecking train succeeded in getting the track clear by Sunday evening."[11]

While this report is not of a wreck involving a flanger car (although Monastery is in the area of Havre Boucher), it may be that the details were confused with other accidents described in the same issue of the *Casket*, connected to the same storm (italics added for emphasis):

"Blizzard. – Nova Scotia had a real blizzard on Tuesday and Thursday night. The strong wind from the northeast, which veered around to the northwest, and which continued throughout the day and night, was accompanied by a heavy snowstorm. The snow drifted and banked up the roads and railway. In many places the snow lies piled some eight feet high. Traffic on the I.C.R, in eastern Nova Scotia was entirely suspended for over twenty-four hours, no trains having reached Antigonish from either the west or east since four o'clock Tuesday afternoon, when the early regular passenger train arrived, being then three hours late, until last evening at 7 p.m., when the regular express from the west reached here. Tuesday's fast express from Sydney did not arrive here until 11 o'clock Wednesday evening, it having been stalled at River Dennis [sic], where the snow plow of the fast freight train had jumped the track and laid until yesterday afternoon. Tuesday's fast express from Halifax did not leave Richmond. Both the east and west fast express trains of Wednesday were cancelled. A snow plough jumped the track at Shubenacadie, on Tuesday, causing much delay to travel between Halifax and Truro. The various stage lines find it impossible to proceed with their trips, and yesterday did not attempt to do so. The storm is certainly the worst of its kind experienced in many years. It will be some days ere travel can be generally resumed."[12]

There is, however, another explanation for the events at Whiteside, resulting from the willingness of society to believe in such things. There have been other notable and documented cases of the poltergeist phenomenon in the United States and Great Britain, corresponding to the era of the Whiteside incident, the oldest of which dates back to Tennessee in 1820, and was witnessed by future president Andrew Jackson.

The so-called Bell Witch haunting did not come to prominence until it was reported in the *Goodspeed History of Tennessee* published in 1886. This coincides with the era in which the haunting of the Fox sisters became widely known, after Margaretta Fox of Hydesville, New York – outraged by the way in which a sister (Leah) had commercially exploited the apparent powers of a medium she and sister Kate possessed – appeared publicly at the New York Academy of Music on October 21st 1888. Margaretta showed how the supposed eerie noises that had accompanied their séances were in fact produced by the surreptitious cracking of knuckles and tapping of feet. The women had developed a strong and loyal following which had coalesced into the Spiritualism movement, and despite the book *The Death-Blow to Spiritualism* by Reuben Briggs Davenport (G. W. Dillingham, 1888), they were still supported by the likes of Sir Arthur Conan Doyle, creator of Sherlock Holmes.

Kate Fox did not participate in the exposé, and would not comment on sister Margaretta's "confession." It was soon discovered that the two, desperate for money that had beem siphoned off by sister Leah, had agreed to the demonstration and accepted $1,500 from a reporter in return for the exclusive right to the story. The two women used the money to support their alcohol addiction, but Margaretta recanted her confession before she died penniless in 1895.

In the same era, Britain's most famous haunting, that at Borley Rectory in Essex, came to the public's attention. The hauntings began in 1885, near the site of an old monastary that was said to have been the venue of a thwarted love between a monk and a nun in the fourteenth century. The paranormal events were first observed in 1885, and stories of bells ringing and lights going on and off would persist for four decades, becoming widely reported in the 1920s by the London *Daily Mirror*, still reknowned for its tabloid style of journalism. The house was destroyed by a mysterious fire in 1939. All three accounts were, therefore, fairly recent to the Whiteside events, and raise the possibility that the Cape Breton incident was a case of small-scale mass hysteria, with liquor as the catalyst.

Poltergeists were not unheard of in Nova Scotia, however; indeed one of them was made famous in Walter Hubbell's 1879 book, *The Great Amherst Mystery: A True Narrative of the Supernatural*, which included an affidavit signed by sixteen witnesses to the haunting of Esther Cox in Amherst, in 1878. Hubbell, who lived with the family – at their request – for six weeks, was forthright in his introduction of the topic:

"No person has yet been able to ascertain their cause. Scientific men from all parts of Canada and the United States have investigated them in vain. Some people think that electricity is the principal agent; others, mesmerism; whilst others again, are sure they are produced by the devil. Of the three supposed causes, the latter is certainly the most plausible theory, for some of the manifestations are remarkably devilish in their appearance and effect. For instance, the mysterious setting of fires, the powerful shaking of the house, the loud and incessant noises and distinct knocking, as if made by invisible sledge-hammers, on the walls; also, the strange actions of the household furniture, which moves about in the broad daylight without the slightest visible cause."[13]

Cox, who died Esther Cox Shanahan at Boston in 1912, was said to have been the victim of a rape at the age of nineteen. Shortly thereafter, ghostly manifestations began to frequent the house on Princess Street, where she lived with her uncle. The poltergeist phenomena included small fires, voices, and rapping noises, which escalated into episodes where Cox would inflate like a balloon. These events were witnessed by many people, who soon made them widely known, so much so that Cox went on tour in 1879, hoping to make money from the phenomena that accompanied her. Exposed as a fraud by the manger of a rival to the theatre where she was performing one night, and later charged with arson by a man whose barn burned when she visited his home, Cox soon slipped from the public eye when she was sentenced to four months in prison on the arson charge.

There was, however, an even more recent event, closer to home. Caledonia Mills in Antigonish County is still an isolated community, and in the 1920s, given the state of Nova Scotia's secondary roads, it was considered very remote, in much the same way that Whiteside is today. Caledonia Mills was the location of the farm of Alexander and Mary MacDonald and their adopted sixteen-year-old daughter, Mary-Ellen. In January of 1922, a fire started in part of their house, but nowhere near the stove that was burning to keep the winter cold at bay.[14] Each time the blaze was extinguished, another erupted in an empty room at the other end of the home. To the family's amazement, and growing concern, even wet cloth and paper would burst into flames.[15]

A close watch by neighbours could not prevent a total of thirty fires that would have been blamed upon an arsonist, had they managed to capture someone in the act. As word leaked out of the community, reporters from across North America took note of the story, and in time, perhaps as a measure of social attitudes towards adoption at the time, suspicion began to fall upon Mary-Ellen.[16] She was blamed for other mysterious occurrences at the farm, including the discovery of ashes in the stored milk, and animals moved from one spot in the barn to another. Mary-Ellen became known as "Mary-Ellen Spook," and the family moved out of the house.[17]

When she moved to Central Canada the incidents ceased, but the fascination with the story has continued to this day. Would-be ghost hunters and parapsychologists of varying degrees of expertise still visit the site.

CHAPTER 6

The Upper Tantallon Ghost

"He was cut down by an engine, sir. No man in England knew his work better. But somehow he was not clear of the outer rail. It was just at broad day. He had struck the light, and had the lamp in his hand. As the engine came out of the tunnel, his back was towards her, and she cut him down." [1]

- Charles Dickens, *Three Ghost Stories*

WHEN the railway station on the old Halifax & Southwestern Railway (H&SW) line at Upper Tantallon[2] was put on the market in 2005, one of the features considered attractive to the sale was the story that it was haunted by the ghost of a station master who died at his post after having been struck by a passing train. According to the story in the now-defunct *Halifax Daily News* of June 6th 2005, which quotes the building's owner:

"The ghost in the attic, however, is priceless.

'I've been told by an old railway man that a station agent was walking down the tracks – I have a feeling he might have been into his cups a bit – and was hit by a train and died...'

...According to local lore, the agent sometimes returns to haunt his old station, dragging an injured foot across the attic floor.

'I feel in my bones it is true because I do hear someone up there,' she said. 'But he's a good ghost. If I go upstairs, I don't hear it'."[3]

The owner has since declined to provide any details, which may be to protect the building from becoming "stigmatized property," a realtor's term to describe a normal building that has become locally famous because of a murder or suicide committed in it. A building believed to be haunted is also stigmatized property, and although the buyer may not care about it, a stigmatized property could be difficult to resell.

With this story, however, a singular lack of detail that would tend to confirm the incident makes it difficult to find any corroborating information from the usual sources.

Railways are creatures of exacting detail, and every incident, accident, and complaint, every piece of freight and baggage was recorded. Newspapers have traditionally been a prime source for such details, for editors recognized and often opposed the political influences that were frequently brought to bear on railway operations in Nova Scotia.

There is a report of one death of an employee at Upper Tantallon station. In her 2001 history of the region, Barbara J. Peart makes note of the tragedy:

"Another railroader, James Simeon Mason, basically laid down his life for the job he loved so dearly. This tragic story was related by his daughter, Iona Agnes (Mason)

Romans, b. August 19, 1912. Lamenting the dismal sadness she had to endure at the tender age of fifteen, Iona stated her father, along with a young lad, Tom Fenerty, and her brother Russell, then eighteen, were on a motorized trolley car out at Bear River Crossing new near (?) Lewin (sic) ledge ("Beachcomber Enterprises Ltd."). Suddenly Russell looked up and saw a train flying towards them! Frantically shouting to his dad to make a jump, he and younger Tom leapt from the trolley to the side of the rails. Simeon thought he had enough time to put the trolley in reverse and back it off to safety, but the train slammed into the trolley before he completed his mission, thus ending his life on July 26 1927; Simeon was 58 years of age. Ironically some years later on December 21, 1961, when Russell Lawrence [Mason] was clearing the tracks in a snowstorm at Rockingham, he, too, was killed by a train."[4]

There is nothing to suggest this might be the origin of the ghost at Upper Tantallon; certainly no station agent or drunkenness was involved. There are, however, enough common elements in the prevailing legend to lend credence to the story. Certainly drunkenness was a common curse of the railway profession, as has been shown in previous chapters of this work. The rules against the habit pre-dated the Halifax & Southwestern's birth and induction into the government system, but railway men were just as quick to take steps to curb the habit. The H&SW employees were members of unions that had sobriety as a main principle in their codes of conduct, as noted by Helen Marot in *American Labor Unions*:

"The brotherhoods have depended on their conservatism for their growth. Their tenets as well as their history are testimonials to their faith in established institutions. They lay stress on the personal conduct of their members, and make no complaints against the exploitation of a class. The cardinal principles of the Brotherhood of Locomotive Engineers are 'sobriety, truth, justice, and morality.' A brother may be expelled from membership for intoxication, the keeping of a saloon or attending a bar, for habitual gambling or for making money through a gambling house. The preamble includes a statement recognizing the need for coordination of capital and labor, and the cultivation of amicable relations with employers. The motto of the Firemen is 'protection, charity, sobriety, and industry.' They also declare their belief in the identity of interests between worker and employer, the necessity of cooperation and the cultivation of harmony. The Brotherhood of Trainmen affirms its intention of establishing mutual confidence and harmonious relations; and its rules of conduct, as well as the rules of the Conductors' Order, are emphatic and strenuous mandates which members disobey at risk of membership."[5]

Stories of drunkenness were easy charges to throw at any railway man by passengers or customers who were dissatisfied with their treatment, or with some real or imagined slight by the railway itself. This was especially true for the local station agent. This occurred at least once, in 1885, and the incident is recorded in G.R. Stevens' history of Canadian National Railways, although without any real evidence.

Stevens' researchers noted that the Intercolonial Railway letter books of October 1885 held correspondence containing allegations of drunkenness of the stationmaster at Elmsdale. (It is not clear if this was in Nova Scotia or Prince Edward Island.)[6] An investigation was held, in which 23 witnesses testified and some 72 pages of evidence were recorded. The stationmaster was exonerated.

What is unusual about the Upper Tantallon phantom, however, is that station agents are rarely subjects of such ghost stories. North American lore abounds with stories of ghost engineers who stay with their runaway trains, conductors who sacrifice their lives to save passengers, brakemen who brave the elements and the speed of their train to slow it from a ride into doom, spirit signal men who wave lamps at the dead of night or during inclement weather…even tramps who meet their end on the ill-fated trains on which they bum a ride, but rarely does the station agent "return" from the dead. This is not to suggest that the job had no romance attached to it. Station agents, especially in the mid 19th Century, were often central figures in the life of small communities, and in many cases stood higher in the social pantheon than a mayor or minister of the church. Writing in 1904, J.J. Shanley said of the master of the small railway station:

"The president of our land, the most exalted of all potentates, is relieved of much of his great responsibility by his cabinet, the supreme judiciary, house and senate, governors, State legislatures, the thinking citizen and the conscientious voter; the commanding general of the army has his staff and numerous subordinates down to the tried and true rank and file; the admiral has his captains, cadets, marines, the men behind the guns and the stanch cruisers themselves; the presidents of the mighty steel arteries of traffic have their vice-presidents, general managers, general superintendents, division superintendents, chief dispatchers, train masters, yard masters, train men, down to the last, but not least, the man with the pick and shovel and spike maul. But the agent at a way station, responsible alike for lives and property, bends alone under his onerous burden. He stands for all that is required from station master, agent, chief clerk, bill clerk, baggage master, ticket agent, express agent, telegraph operator and general factotum.

The station itself is regarded and utilized as a public building; the agent is the chief personage in the immediate community, as well as in the burgs and hamlets contiguous and tributary thereto. He is at once the slave and idol of every man, woman and child for miles around. He is the confidant of all the gossips and is unwillingly cognizant of the dangling skeletons in the rural closets. He is the butt of all the trainmen as well as the subject of complimentary comments at every session of the "Stove Committee." His time, early and late, seven days in the week and every day in the year, is devoted to the company's interests and the welfare of its patrons, with never a thought for himself, as he has no affairs and is known to his children as that man who sleeps part of the night at their house."[7]

It also cannot be said that the H&SW could not have been the setting for such a tragedy as that suggested by the Upper Tantallon ghost. In its ninety-year history the railway had its fair share of devastating and fatal accidents.

Projections for the railway began in 1897, when Yarmouth Steamship Company saw its business slowly being taken from it by the aggressive marketing of the Dominion Atlantic Railway. It was not until 1902, however, that William Mackenzie and Donald Mann began to stitch together the small railways on Nova Scotia's south shore into a 320-kilometre (200 mile) line from Yarmouth to Halifax, the largest piece of which was completed in 1904 between Bridgewater and Halifax. These lines included the Nova Scotia Central Railway, the Coast Railway, Granville Valley & Victoria Beach Railway, Halifax & Yarmouth Railway, Liverpool & Milton Railway, Middleton & Victoria

Above: The former H&SW station at French Village, as it appeared at the turn of the century, shortly after the railway line was opened in 1905.
(Courtesy private collection)

Beach Railway, Nictaux & Atlantic Railway and the Nova Scotia, Nictaux & Atlantic Central Railway. McKenzie and Mann were the principals of the Canadian Northern Railway (CNoR), with aspirations to build a second transcontinental line to compete against the Canadian Pacific Railway (CPR). The plan ultimately failed, and the CNoR was taken over by the federal government and merged with the Intercolonial in 1922 into what would become known as the Canadian National Railways. Despite its short existence as a privately owned line, the employees of the H&SW resisted attempts to identify themselves by the Intercolonial and CNR names, always referring to themselves as employees of the "Hellish, Slow & Wobbly"!

Among the more infamous – and spectacular – wrecks, the railway can number the collision at Mahone Junction in February of 1907, when three men perished after a freight train collided with a passenger train, wrecking the Mahone freight shed and strewing lumber in all directions. The Bridgewater *Bulletin* of February 12th takes up the story:

"A special freight train from Bridgewater for Lunenburg with 14 cars of lumber, in charge of Conductor Driscoll and Driver Barteaux of Engine No. 1, lost control of the air-brakes on the grade between blockhouse and Mahone Junction, and rushed through the switch which had been left open for the train to Halifax, which was shortly due, and crashed into the engine of the Lunenburg-Middleton train then standing at the station. Conductor Driscoll had left his train on the top of the grade and went forward to close the switch and direct his train on the Lunenburg track, but before he got to the switch the train rushed past him and the collision occurred.

Driver Barteaux and Fireman Lynch JUMPED AND WERE SAVED.

Driver William Phalen and Fireman Enos Crooks who were on the engine at the station were hurled some distance, Crooks landing under the platform. He was so terribly injured that he died in about two hours. Phalen had his left leg torn off just about the knee, and the right leg sustained a compound fracture. Willis W. Lowe, a section foreman, was standing in front of the freight shed and was crushed to death by flying lumber and freight cars. Two other men who were standing near warned Crooks to fly for his life but he did not heed. The others jumped and avoided injury.

Why Phalen and Crooks did not jump when the runaway freight approached cannot be understood. There was sufficient warning as the driver of the freight train whistled the alarm until he jumped, and the distance from the switch to where No. 3 was standing would give ample time for the men to jump to safety."[8]

Faulty airbrakes, a device recently introduced to improve safety, were cited as the cause of the accident, as was the overloading of the No. 5 train. The newspaper described the accident as the worst that had occurred on the railway at that time, but the events of February 24th 1911 near Caledonia, on the old Nova Scotia Central Railway line, would soon supersede it. In that accident, according to the Bridgewater *Bulletin* of February 28th 1911:

Below: French Village station (now Tantallon) as it was in 1987, prior to the abandonment of the line by Canadian National Railways.
(Courtesy Eugene D. Burleson)

"…The south bound train from Port Wade and Middleton met with a serious accident. At New Germany Junction the baggage and mail car, one passenger car, two box and a flat car left the track and toppled over an embankment. In the baggage and mail car were baggage man McLaughlin and mail clerk Jackson and brakeman Archie MacDonald."[9]

There were nineteen passengers on the train; all escaped with various injuries, but the crew did not fare as well. The brakeman was instantly killed; Baggageman Orren McLaughlin was left in the baggage car when the others were rescued and his remains were not recovered for more than a day after the wreck.[10]

Perhaps the most fabled wreck on the line, involved spirits, but fortunately no loss of life. It occurred at Ingramport on November 16th 1974. In the evening of that day, a Canadian National Railways freight train of two locomotives and seven boxcars was running from Bridgewater to the yard at Rockingham in Halifax, when it derailed on an open switch at Ingramport, on what had by then become the Chester Subdivision.

Among the derailed cars were two that were loaded with bottles of whisky and other spirits, loaded at the Bridgetown distillery in the Annapolis Valley. The news of the wreck quickly spread. Since the scene was only a short walk from Highway 3, a throng of spectators gathered to view the proceedings, and attempted to mount their own rescue mission: to retrieve the mostly intact cargo of liquor from the boxcars. Despite the best efforts of CN's police force, it is said that a number of unbroken bottles disappeared into the night, finding new lives in private hands. Most of the remaining bottles were dispatched the following day when they were crushed under a bulldozer and buried. Local rumor claims even some of those spirits rose again!

The Upper Tantallon ghost raises an interesting aspect of Nova Scotia's long tradition of haunted houses and supernatural phenomena, because there is nothing in the province's regulations pertaining to stigmatized properties, at least where ghosts are concerned. The regulations only call for the realtor to disclose any factual information pertaining to a property that a reasonable person would consider relevant to a consumer's decision to buy.

Another incident related in Peart's history of the community might also offer foundation to the Upper Tantallon ghost. Typically, such ghosts are associated with devastating wrecks and death on-the-job, such as those at Mahone Junction and Caledonia, but could it be that this ghost is actually that of an employee who loved his work, and was determined never to miss a day of it…even after retirement and death?

"Eugene MacLean, son of David and Matilda, (b. abt. 1887; d. Dec. 13,1965 at age 78) acquired a job with C.N.R. after he was released from the army in World War II and worked on the railroad until he retired. He drove his bicycle back and forth to work to the station, and people could set their watches by his travels up and down the road. One day he had an unfortunate accident on his bike. Cora Nash said he had a bad accident and was bleeding very badly. The people brought him into her house and laid him on the kitchen floor until the ambulance arrived."[11]

Is the Upper Tantallon ghost Eugene MacLean, walking his beat by the tracks? And how factual can any ghost claim be? In the case of this station, surely that depends upon the prospective buyer's willingness to believe the story, just as the readers of this work are expected to base their conclusions on the facts that are available in each case.

CHAPTER 7

Dealing with the Devil!

Well a railway man lay dying with his people by his side
His family were crying, knelt in prayer before he died
But above his bed just a-waiting for the dead
Was the Devil with a twinkle in his eye
"Well God's not around and look what I've found
This one's mine"

- Chris De Burgh, "The Spanish Train"

I N the final story of his second book of Maritime mysteries, Bill Jessome made note of a satanic visit to New Glasgow:

"Having just been paid, some railroaders headed for the shack where they gathered around an old table for a hand or two of poker. One young player was on a lucky streak and kept winning with a pair of deuces. He boasted that he was so hot he could even beat the devil."[1]

Jessome notes the young man got his chance when a stranger entered the shack and asked to join the game. The newcomer soon began winning every hand, and in a fit of pique at losing repeatedly, the young card sharp threw down his losing hand, scattering his cards on the floor. Bending down to pick them up, he noticed the stranger's long black cloak was hiding cloven hooves:

"When the young man looked into his black, piercing eyes, a cold chill went through him. The stranger then turned into a ball of fire, and went straight through the roof of the old shack. No matter how many times the hole was repaired, it would mysteriously appear again."[2]

The story, as Tom Knapp has noted in his critique of Jessome's first volume of mysteries, is sadly lacking in detail, not the least of which is that it is a variation of a traditional theme. In her 1975 work, *Folklore of Nova Scotia*, Mary L. Fraser records an identical story from Creignish in Cape Breton[3]. Jessome's story, however, does contain elements common to both supernatural superstition and traditional railroad lore.

The first is the connection between the devil and card games (although it should be noted the original Spanish folk tale, popularized in DeBurgh's song, had God and the Devil playing chess for the souls of the dead, not poker.) Those opposed to gaming and gambling on religious grounds have called a deck of cards "The Devil's Bible" or "The Devil's Picture Book" since the 1300s, and at various times in both Europe and North America, have opposed the use of cards with the zeal employed by the temperance movement against alcohol. (This same attitude is alive today in opposition to the popularity of some video games being sold to children.)

Bible tracts produced for distribution among railway workers warned of the "sinful fruits" that would be reaped by engaging in both gambling and the use of alcohol. In the 1920s, such warnings were issued using gambling as a metaphor for the rampant stock market speculation that was going on until the market crashed in October of 1929, bringing on the "Dirty Thirties."

Writing in 1904, on the history of the railroad division of the Young Men's Christian Association (established in Cleveland, Ohio in 1872), G.J. Warburton wrote:

"One test that has always been applied has been the ability of the association to keep railroad employees out of the saloon, the brothel and the gambling resort. Railroading in the old days attracted a type of men to whom vices of various kinds made a strong appeal. It was a common thing for them to be woefully lacking in good morals. Many were dissolute, and the location of a terminal in a town was considered a calamity because of the undesirable men who would thus be brought into it. It is also true that the restraints that are around the workingman of the same social grade in other employment are lacking in a railroad man's life. His hours are generally irregular. Much of his time must be spent away from home. His labour is exhausting to physical and nervous force to such an extent that the desire for stimulants is stronger in its appeal than it might otherwise be. Yet the nature of his responsibility is such that he must be alert, sober, trustworthy."[4]

Warburton's concern was for the influence of drink and gambling; nothing was said of making the workplace safer.

The young New Glasgow worker's winning hand of a pair of deuces (twos of any suit) in Jessome's story also evokes the use of the word "deuce" in two senses, the first being that of bad luck. It was derived from the French word for two, "deux," in that a throw of two on a pair of dice was the lowest possible score. The second use of "deuce" originated with the Low German word "duus," the Devil, and has been used since the mid-seventeenth century as a polite reference to Satan, made in mixed company or by those who would be considered gentlemen. In the nineteenth century "deuce" became synonymous for "damn."

The idea that the devil created the explosion at New Glasgow may, however, have been nothing more than a railwayman's flippant explanation for an event that was all too common – and a symptom of a tacit abrogation of responsibility. Certainly such events were not mysterious, as the Moncton *Daily Transcript* of December 2nd 1920 recorded:

"A gasoline tank blew up in the C.N.R. shops today, going through the roof. Officials stated that no person was injured, as none were near the tank at the time of the explosion, it was reported that the tank in its assent went through several skylights. Another official when asked concerning the explosion, said, "It isn't worth mentioning.""[5]

The Daily Times of Moncton found it worth mentioning a second time, however, noting a new source for the event in its December 3rd edition:

Above: The Intercolonial Railway (CNR) station at New Glasgow, Nova Scotia, as seen in a postcard published before the fire of 1923.
(Jay Underwood collection)

"The explosion of an oxygen tank in the Canadian National Railway shops yesterday afternoon about 2 o'clock caused some excitement among the employees.

No loss of life was caused by the explosion, neither were there any injuries. The facts of the case are that the tank was placed in its position apart from the shops building and that a separate shed was built for the same. No one was near when the explosion took place but is expected that an examination of the case will prove that no one was injured.

The building containing the tank was apart from the main shops and was some twelve or fifteen feet high. The explosion was sufficient to blow the roof off the small building where the tank was situated, also to blow the windows off the nearby shops. Other than that no damage was done."[6]

It wasn't the first time that such an occurrence had been taken lightly. The *Canadian National Railways Magazine* of March 1919 reported:

"The Moncton fire department was called out one evening to extinguish a fire in the trackmen's shanty. It was thought at first that the incendiary language of the yard foreman caused the fire, on account of the McAdoo award not having been put into effect, but it was later learned that the cause was an overheated stove. Very slight damage was done."[7]

(The McAdoo Award was the ruling laid down in 1918 by William Gibbs McAdoo, Secretary of the US Treasury and director of the US Railroad Administration that gave American railway workers higher wage increases, and prevented unionized workers from being discriminated against. Because of the international operations of Canadian National Railway and Canadian Pacific Railway, they were obliged to follow suit.)

The 1919 shanty fire was by no means an isolated event, and Moncton – the headquarters of the Intercolonial Railway, and regional headquarters for Canadian National Railways after 1922 – was frequently the venue for such spectacles, as the Moncton *Times* reported in its February 16th 1925 edition:

"Mystery surrounds the cause of an explosion which occurred about one o'clock this morning and partially wrecked the C.N.R. Switchmen's shanty near the Main Street Subway.

Aubrey Steeves, switchman on duty was in the shanty at the time but he was not injured. The force of the explosion was considerable as the windows of the shanty were blown out and the window frames split while several of the clapboards on the back and sides were blown off, some of them being shot clear across the street to the lot on which the Royal Lunch car stands. The patrons in the lunch car at the time also state the car was shaken by the explosion."[8]

This explosion was made even more mysterious by the lack of any gas used in the immediate area, leading to the conclusion that it had been caused by a build up of gasses from ashes that had been placed beneath the floor of the shanty the previous fall.

This event sounds eerily similar to that of Jessome's story, and had he done the research required by Knapp, it would have discovered that the New Glasgow event – which Jessome records only as happening in the "early twenties" – does have some factual basis, for the town's station was burned on March 7th 1923, as the *Eastern Chronicle* of March 9th noted:

"One of the most important buildings in New Glasgow, fell prey to a fire early on Wednesday morning, when the large Railway Station was almost completely destroyed. The four brick walls are standing, but the interior is completely gutted and destroyed.

It was about two o'clock on Wednesday morning when Night Dispatcher James Ryan smelled smoke and went out in the narrow hall that ran the length of the second floor to investigate. He found that a fire had broken out in or near the ladies' waiting room and had gained considerable headway. It had complete possession of the single stairway and cut off his chances of exit in that direction. He promptly sent in an alarm and was later rescued from his position by the aid of a ladder extended to the roof that he reached from one of the windows. The firemen instantly answered the alarm and they early had no les than seven streams of water under high pressure playing into the building, but the fire had so much the upper hand that a deluge would have made little impression upon it. The long upper hall and an open attic above the whole length of the structure materially contributed to a good fire on the second floor. From the first floor considerable material was saved, such as the contents of the ticket office and lower telegraph office and men's waiting room, but as far as further occupancy is concerned they are out of the question."[9]

The cause of this fire had also never been determined, but an over-heated furnace was considered to be the most likely source. The newspaper played down the sensation of the razing of a building so important to the affairs of a small town, but in doing so, may have unwittingly created another element to supernatural events: "At no time was the fire a spectacular one, though it blazed fiercely and was of that obdurate type, hard to root out. But few citizens failed to respond to the continued ringing of the fire alarm which banged out a succession of thirteens for well over half an hour."[10] One need not attach much importance to the occurrence of the numbers seven (a lucky number) in the date, and thirteen (an unlucky number; the fire alarms were sounded giving the Morse code for the number) to this event, or the two (deux) o'clock outbreak of the blaze on the second floor, but they are difficult to ignore.

The twenties saw several major fires at CNR facilities in the region – including New Glasgow, Moncton, and Bridgewater – for which Satan could not always be blamed. Workplace safety was still in its infancy in the railway industry, and despite the fact it was preached regularly in the Canadian National Railways Magazine, the message often went unheeded. Every edition routinely offered advice such as "You need not be an artist to draw a Safety score," or "Work for Safety means Safety in work," and "Safety means more than property, it means LIFE; perhaps your life or that of one of your family." Regrettably these warnings were frequently ignored.

Indeed, in the 1920s, the notion of the "professional" railway man was still very new to many of the employees. Writing in the *Scientific American* of February 17th 1912 in

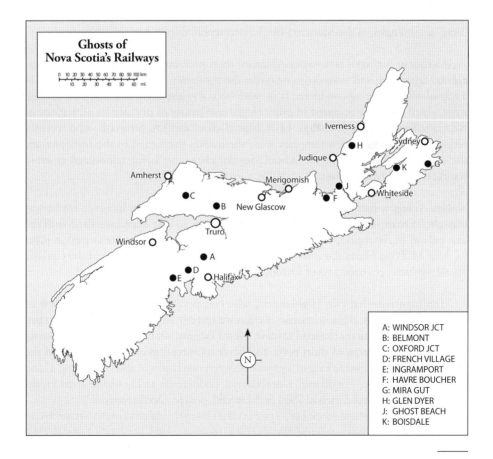

Ghosts of
Nova Scotia's Railways

0 10 20 30 40 50 60 70 80 90 100 km
   10   20   30   40   50   60   mi.

Iverness

Sydney

H

Judique

K

G

Amherst

Merigomish

C

J

B   New Glascow

F

Whiteside

Truro

Windsor

A

D

E   Halifax

N

A: WINDSOR JCT
B: BELMONT
C: OXFORD JCT
D: FRENCH VILLAGE
E: INGRAMPORT
F: HAVRE BOUCHER
G: MIRA GUT
H: GLEN DYER
J: GHOST BEACH
K: BOISDALE

his article "How Railroad Men are Made: Training the Men Who Run Big Railways", author Paul Harvey Middleton noted:

"The Canadian Pacific, at its Angus works in Montreal, has also recently inaugurated a new system of training employees; and in order to encourage deserving apprentices, the company donates each year a scholarship to the best ten apprentices, consisting of complete courses in mechanical or electrical engineering. The railroad also awards two scholarships, tenable for four years at McGill University, Montreal."[11]

Prior to this, all a railway worker had needed to succeed and advance in his career was a strong back, quick wits, and a willingness to work long hard hours. They also frequently had cavalier attitudes towards the inherent danger of their work. Many of the accidents common to the Intercolonial and Canadian National Railways in the 1920s involved men who had been long-time employees, and while some advanced their professional education through correspondence school, many had not received the formal safety training the younger apprentices were then getting.

These calamities were occurring at a time when railway employees, who had been accustomed to working with and handling wood, coal, and tallow, found themselves dealing with highly flammable substances like oxygen, acetylene, and gasoline. Many of them found themselves having a "deuce" of a time with it! For that reason, Canadian National Railways instituted an educational program aimed directly at veteran workers forced to deal with the "new" technologies, as the Moncton *Daily Times* reported in its May 9th 1929 edition:

"Canadian National Railway conductors, trainmen, engineers, firemen, operators, agents, signal men and others coming under the regulations are now being instructed at a school which is being conducted here, with both day and night classes, in the revised rules which are being adopted in order to get uniformity of practice on all regions of the Canadian National Railways. J.F.R. MacMichael and J.A. Stronach, who recently returned from Montreal where they were themselves instructed in the revisions, are the instructors in the Moncton school. Similar classes are being conducted at every terminal point in the region."[12]

New Glasgow had a more historic connection with Beelzebub, however, for he was thought by many denizens of the Pictou County town to have been associated with the first railway in the region, established at Albion Mines (now nearby Stellarton) in 1839.

Amy M. Pope relates the story in her article "Antigonish", published in the *Catholic World*, (volume 40, issue 235) of October, 1884:

"Tradition tells that two Highlanders, who had never before seen that triumph of modern mechanism, the locomotive, were once terribly frightened by this coal-train. They were walking along the road towards New Glasgow, when suddenly with a hoarse roar followed by a series of short puffs, this black monster appeared to come out of the earth, and crawled slowly along in a groove between two banks of ashes, dragging a long line of "coal-hoppers." "Seall! seall! Dondill, seall, tiodhlacadh an Diobhail!" cried Sandy, which being interpreted means, "See! See! Donald, see the Devil's funeral!"[13]

CHAPTER 8

Roundhouse Ghosts

No exorciser harm thee!
Nor no witchcraft charm thee!
Ghost unlaid forbear thee!
Nothing ill come near thee!
Quiet consummation have;
And renowned be thy grave!

- William Shakespeare, "Fidele"

ROUNDHOUSE ghosts – such as that seen in the Moncton shops associated with locomotive No. 239, the "hoodooed engine" of the first chapter – are not uncommon in the lore of any railway. Some have been proven to be demonstrably false. Or have they?

When the Monon Railroad in the United States (now a long-fallen flag) was the major route for Kentucky coal bound for Indiana steel mills in the 1920s, so strong was the belief in the existence of a ghost in the roundhouse at Monon – the small town from which the line took its name – that veteran railroaders considered walking off the job until something was done about the spook.[1] Police laid the blame on two drunken teenagers on a nearby hill, who had rigged up a sheet over a balloon and manipulated it with a string. Many workers were unconvinced; the ghost had been seen wandering inside the building, something the imagination and dexterity of even the most sober of miscreants could not have managed.

In his first book of regional ghost stories, Bill Jessome offers a brief account of a phantom that haunted the old roundhouse of the Sydney & Louisburg Railway on Cape Breton Island.[2] (Such is the nature of Jessome's work, that it must be noted the reference to the roundhouse is misleading. There was only one such building on the line, the true round engine house at Glace Bay. The sheds at Whitney Pier and Louisbourg were also called roundhouses, but did not have that unique shape.)

The Sydney & Louisburg began with faltering steps in 1877, as the local coal mines attempted to make Louisbourg – recognized as the premier ice-free port on the east coast (and the closest to Great Britain by several days over Halifax) – the terminus of a railway that would eventually rival the Intercolonial's ambition to span the nation. Small coal railways proliferated in the Sydney region, of various gauges and merit, and it was not until the Dominion Steel Company (DOSCO) was established by an amalgamation of these operations in 1893 that the S&L took on a more definite indentity. The railway reached Louisbourg in 1895. With the addition of a steel mill at Whitney Pier in 1901 and more coal mines, the line's future seemed much more assured than so many Nova Scotia railways predicated on less stable financial ground. (Historians commonly make note of the serendipitous spelling of Louisburg, as opposed to the French name of the community that the railway served, Louisbourg.)

By 1890, however, the Intercolonial had reached Sydney. This relegated the S&L to short line status from which it never recovered, because the steel industry underwent a series of corporate transformations following the First World War. The line developed its own unique character, however, as Robert Chant has observed in his on-line history:

"The S&L was a neighbourly and unpretentious railroad, and it operated on a personal basis that meant a lot to the people it served. The railroad ran picnic excursions and 'blueberry specials' that would stop anywhere to let passengers off, and pick them up in the evening. It took little for a hunter or vacationer to flag a train and get on, and the crews always took a lively interest in the latest news along the line. Many times, often in foul weather and blizzards, the S&L sent out a locomotive and car to take a doctor somewhere, or bring someone into hospital. There may have been more pranks and practical jokes played by S&L men than on any other line in the country, but they were tough and competent railroaders – in the early days, before air brakes, they spent many runs climbing over the icy tops of coal hoppers to brake the trains – and they moved an enormous amount of coal."[3]

By that time, the railway operated more than 116 miles of track, thirty-nine of which could be considered "main line," and was carrying more than four million tons of coal and general freight annually. It also provided a heavily-used passenger service between the two termini and the suburbs and Sydney. Most of the passengers were miners; their numbers peaked at 176,000 in 1913, a volume that would be the envy of many similar sized railways elsewhere on the contintent.[4] Long before it became the Cape Breton Development Corporation's (DEVCO) property in 1967, the S&L was billed as "busiest railway in North America."

Following the Second World War, however, the S&L suffered with other lines from the competition offered by automobiles and the increased mechanization of the mining industry. World steel prices later began to fall as foreign markets began producing at cheaper rates. The S&L survived the new market with dogged determination; in the 1950s, according to Brian Campbell's 1995 history, its steam roster held thirty-one locomotives with a payroll of more than 400 employees.[5]

It could not survive the acquisition by the British firm of Hawker-Siddley, which invested heavily in several Nova Scotia steel mills and shipyards after 1957, only to have them fail and close amid dire predictions that the Cape Breton coal industry had a mere fifteen years of useful resources left. The acquisition of deisel engines in 1961 was merely the harbinger of the end of the line, and the last steam locomotive went out of service in 1966. The creation of the Cape Breton Develoment Corporation (DEVCO) to take over operation of the coal mines in 1967 (the steel mills were taken over by the provincially-owned Sydney Steel Corporation, SYSCO) was the death knell. The funeral came in 1968.

Jessome quotes Leo Evans as having being told of the roundhouse ghost after Evans joined S&L in 1942. Foreman Joe R. MacDonald warned him well in advance of the wraith's existence.[6] Evans is a respected local historian of the Whitney Pier area. He told of the occasion when two workers in the roundhouse saw a figure in the cab of an unidentified locomotive that had been left for servicing. When the men investigated,

Above: The 1903 Mira Bridge wreck on Cape Breton Island. Engineer James Parsons may have been one of the few railroaders to drown while on duty.
(Courtesy Sydney & Louisburg Railway Museum)

they found no one in the cab, and no footprints in the snow outside to indicate that anyone had left the engine. In many ways it is a story similar to that of the locomotive in the first part of this work. As Jessome notes: "There were many theories about why the ghost was haunting the place, but no one ever found out."[7]

Jessome unfortunately doesn't offer any details on those theories, and Evans cannot supply any information, but if a ghost is truly the manifestation of the unrequited spirit of an employee who died on the job, the S&L offered several opportunities, for there were many fatalities on the road. This was not because the line was poorly run, or that the employees were overly careless, simply a reflection of the volume of traffic on the "busiest" line on the continent. One of these was fairly typical and took place November 27th 1903. It was reported in the Antigonish *Casket* of December 3rd 1903: "Malcolm MacLean, 21 years old, of Boisdale, a brakeman on the Sydney and Louisburg Railway was instantly killed at Glace Bay by being run over in the yard by a car on Friday."[8]

It was the final fatal accident of a year that had not begun well for the railway. James Parson had died in the most spectacular wreck, on April 15th 1903, as reported in the Moncton *Daily Times*:

"A serious accident occurred this morning at Mira Gut. Engine No. 52, a 110-ton engine, in charge of Engineer James Parson and fireman Dickson, was coming up from

Louisburg with a train of seventy empty cars. The drawbridge at Mira gut was open, and the flag was out. Owing probably to the fact that this is unusual so early in the year it was unnoticed by the driver, and the engine was close to the draw before they noticed that it was open. The fireman jumped but the engineer went down with his engine. The water is about twenty feet deep. In a short time the driver was brought out of the river. He was fifty five years of age, has a wife and family at Louisburg, and has been in the Sydney & Louisburg employ two years."[9]

The fatalities continued at various times, as the Sydney *Daily Post* reported in the June 5th 1920 edition:

"Thomas McDonald age 70 years died in hospital in Glace Bay as a result of being struck by a shunting train on the Sydney & Louisbourg in the biggest town yesterday afternoon. The unfortunate man was returning home from work, when he attempted to cross the railroad tracks. He apparently did not notice the approach of a shunting engine with several cars attached, and before he could get out of danger was knocked down. One leg was so badly crushed that amputation was necessary and Mr. McDonald died three hours after reaching hospital. Four sons survive him, Hughie, Dan, and Angus at home in Glace Bay, Archie in Toronto, Norman in the West, and two daughters Rachel and Christine at home. The deceased was employed in the car shop."[10]

These calamities were not limited to the railway's employees, and one of the round-houses succumbed to the ever-present threat of fire in the year that Thomas McDonald died:

"The Sydney & Louisburg roundhouse at Louisburg was completely destroyed by fire tonight. The fire was discovered about nine o'clock and it made such headway that before an hour the roundhouse was a mass of charred ruins. At the time there were four locomotives in the shop, but the men who were working night shift succeeded in getting them all out. The cab of one engine was completely destroyed, while another was severely damaged.

The firemen appeared on the scene, but the flames had made such progress that they were powerless to check them. The different machine and shop apparatus were saved. The loss is $10,000."[11]

Railroaders were not the only ones to succumb to the dangers of the profession, especially where the Sydney & Louisburg Railway was concerned. The Sydney *Post Record* of June 22nd 1936 reported three weekend fatalities in the Sydney area, one of which claimed the life of Donald R. MacDonald, the 37 year-old chief clerk of the DOSCO comptroller's department. MacDonald died hours after being crushed by thirty cars of a coal train at a private crossing on the King's Road main line, just yards from his home. He had been en route to his home at the time, and after running down a steep and rough incline leading to the crossing, he stumbled when he reached the bottom of the hill, struck his head on the tracks as he fell, and remained there stunned. The train, owned by the Sydney and Louisburg Railway, with a CNR crew in charge, had left the Sydney depot at 3:05 pm and was travelling to Sydney Mines with a string of empty cars.

The body was seen by Hilton Grant, forward brakeman on the engine that was proceeding tender first, when the train was about 50 feet away from it. He immediately signalled to the engineer to stop, but the proximity of the body prohibited all attempts to avoid an accident, and when the train was finally brought to a halt, the horribly broken remains of MacDonald were found lying under the last car. Unconscious, MacDonald was removed from beneath the train and taken to the hospital where he lived for four hours, his death occurring at 7:30 o'clock, Saturday evening. An inquest held at City Hall by Magistrate A. M. Crofton, returned a verdict of accidental death and exonerated the train crew from all blame."[12]

The widespread publicity did nothing to prevent similar tragedies. A year later, the Glace Bay *Coastal Courier* of April 3rd 1937 reported the death of 58 year-old Sydney steelworker Angus MacDonald (not known to be a relative of Donald MacDonald) when he was run down by a locomotive at the steel plant near Prince Street:

"Employed at the steel plant, MacDonald was walking along the tracks on his way to work on the 11 o'clock shift when hit. His screams attracted the notice of one of the brakeman, and when the train was brought to a stop and examination made by the crew, it was found that he was dead.

For a time after the fatality, identity of the victim was unknown, and a number of citizens who viewed the remains offered conjectural opinions, but it was only after the remains were taken to Curry's morgue that identification was definitely established."[13]

Again the train crew could not be found at fault for MacDonald's demise, for as the newspaper reported:

"He was near-sighted and slightly deaf, and apparently failed to hear the train approaching. The train, composed of cars of steel products was bound for Louisburg and was in charge of Conductor Dan Kerr. Immediately after the accident, D.N. MacDonald, superintendent of the Sydney and Louisburg Railway, was notified and rushed to the scene, also Police Officer Don Curry. Curry's ambulance was phoned for, also Dr. W.H. Rice, and subsequently the body of the unfortunate victim taken to the morgue and relatives notified by Police Chief W.R. Tracey. Examining the remains at the scene, Magistrate A.M. Crofton, acting as coroner in the absence of Dr. J.K. MacLeod, who is in New York, ordered an inquest which was held at 10.30 o'clock this morning at city hall."[14]

It was not until almost five years later that a coroner's jury rendered a verdict to prevent such fatalities, as the Sydney *Post Record* reported in its December 6th 1941 edition:

"Severely injured yesterday morning when struck by incoming passenger express while he was walking along the railway main line here, Stephen Steele, 63, died in Saint Rita's Hospital early yesterday afternoon. Horribly mangled about the legs Steele underwent amputation of both limbs after admitted to the hospital and he lived for 90 minutes after the operation. Shock, along with injuries sustained, contributed to his death according to medical testimony.

An inquest held last night before Dr J.K. MacLeod, Coroner, returned a verdict of accidental death, and exoneration of the train crew, but recommends that the railways resume blowing whistles approaching all crossings in the city. Up until about three weeks ago, whistles were sounded by incoming and outgoing trains while traveling through the city limits, the Board of Railway Commissioners following representations made by the City Council.

Narrowly escaping the same fate of Steele, was a fellow worker, James McPhail of King's Road, who was shoved clear of danger after the engine had struck the victim. McPhail received an injured foot and had to be transported to and from City Hall last evening where the coroner's inquiry was held, and had to be assisted in and out of the building to a waiting car."[15]

The unlucky Steele died an hour and half after the accident; both his legs had been amputated, and he never recovered consciousness. There was no evidence of liquor having been consumed by either man. They had walked to work to collect their pay, rather than risk driving the company truck over the icy tracks. The crossing keeper testified that he had shouted warnings to the two men, and that the bells at the crossing were operating, and were audible. The locomotive engineer said he never saw the two men walking ahead of his train.[16] It seemed there was little the locomotive crew could do to avert the disaster:

"MacFarlane, the fireman, said he noticed the two men walking down the spur leading from the warehouse yard, and he said he figured they would walk alongside the rails on reaching the main line, but they did not. He said he noticed that Steele turned around on reaching the main line and kept on walking down the tracks on the inside. It was impossible to avoid the accident by bringing the train to an immediate stop, as the men were about 30 feet distant at the time. The signal bell on the crossing was in operation at the time, the witness stated, and ringing. The inquest jury presided over by Dr J.K. MacLeod, Coroner, and with Neil Johnson, as foreman, deliberated for about five minutes before returning a verdict of accidental death, exoneration of the train crew, and attached to their finding was a recommendation that whistle blowing be resumed by trains approaching all crossings within the city."[17]

If there was indeed a ghost at any of the S&L's roundhouses, there was certainly no shortage of candidates. Any one of these incidents might substantiate the story of the roundhouse spectre, but there are some errors in Jessome's work that tend to add to any doubts about its veracity:

"One of the more frightening encounters happened when a callboy, or dispatcher, was alone in the office. While the boy was on the phone the door opened and the ghost walked in. The callboy wanted to run but he was too scared to move. He knew if he stood up his legs would collapse under him. All he could do was sit there and watch the spectre move about the office. Then as quickly as he came in, the ghost turned, stared at the startled young man for a moment, and left."[18]

Callboys were not dispatchers. They were more often than not youngsters whose job it was to summon the train crews – engineers, firemen, brakemen – to report to work, often at a moment's notice and sometimes after they had just completed a long shift on another train.

Evans offers another theory; that ghost stories began to evolve as television became more widely available, and science fiction was becoming a popular form of story telling.[19] The combination of ancient ghosts and modern technology seems perfectly suited to such stories, and one might suspect this is the case with this roundhouse ghost, except that it had been reported as far back as the 1940s. There was another medium becoming popular at the time Evans found work on the railway. The comic book was giving rise to the popularity of such figures as Batman (1939), the Flash (1940), Green Lantern (1940), and Superman (1940), and radio had been telling stories of the Shadow since 1931. These stories were becoming part of the popular culture, perhaps as an escape from the grim realities of a war that appeared to be without end. It may also be that Evans was "having his leg pulled" by veteran workers at the roundhouse. Perhaps the frequency of so many fatal accidents on so small a railway provided the inevitable grist for ghost stories.

CHAPTER 9

Trains of Evil

"There's a long black train,
Comin' down the line,
Feedin' off the souls that are lost and cryin',
Rails of sin, only evil remains
Watch out brother for that Long Black Train."

- Josh Turner, "Long Black Train"

THE imagery of the long black train has long been used in railway lore as an ominous harbinger of tragedy, death, or destruction, be they real or phantom. Few are the railways in North America that do not have their own ghost or long black trains. The only "ghost train" that was not looked upon with such trepidation was the 1840s-era New York, New Haven & Hartford Railroad's luxurious train of the same name, hauling white cars that ran between New York and Boston for the well-heeled traveller in five hours and ten minutes.

In her 1976 book *Folklore of Nova Scotia*, Mary L. Fraser documented four stories of phantom trains on Cape Breton Island, including the Mabou train on what would become the route of the Inverness & Richmond Railway, discussed in Chapter Four of this work. The first is that of a train seen at Barachois, on the route traced by what would become the Intercolonial from Point Tupper to Sydney:

"Some years ago, people who live on a certain hill at Barrachois, [sic] Cape Breton, used to watch a phantom train glide noiselessly around the headlands of the Bras d'Or and come to a stop at a gate leading to one of the houses. One who saw it for herself told me how at seven o'clock every evening for a whole month, every family on the hill would go out of doors to see it. Every coach was lighted, but people could not be seen. At the hour of the approach, some people sometimes went down to the track to get a better look at it, but were disappointed at its not coming at all, although the watchers on the hill saw it as usual. At the end of the month, a train just at the gate to which the phantom train used to come killed a man. Nobody saw it afterwards."[1]

Fraser's lack of detail makes any corroboration difficult, but it appears, since her sources were all interviewed personally, and were elderly, that these occurrences all took place in the early 1900s, perhaps at the same time that a morbid fascination with death was so prevalent following the passing of Queen Victoria.

Barachois lies on the southern shore of St. Andrew's Channel, as the line weaves its way to Sydney Mines, then doubles back towards Sydney. As that town's coal and steel industries began to grow, traffic on the line through the quiet rural communities increased markedly, as the Halifax *Chronicle* of July 19th 1901 noted when Collingwood

Schreiber, the deputy minister of railways and canals, David Pottinger, general manager of the Intercolonial Railway and his subordinates; E.G. Russell, manager, E. Tiffin, traffic Manager, and W.B. McKenzie, chief engineer, accompanied by their wives and secretaries, arrived in Sydney.[2] Pottinger was quick to refute rumours that the railway was considering transferring its Eastern division headquarters from New Glasgow to Sydney, but plans were being made to enlarge the Sydney depot and yard, as the steel and coal industries blossomed.

With the high officials expressing their confidence in the growth of Sydney, the traffic on the Cape Breton section of the Intercolonial Railway had more than trebled, leaving out the construction material hauled for the Dominion Iron and Steel Company. It was small wonder, then, that the accidents were not limited to the crowded yards of Sydney. The death to which Fraser's sources refer may have been that of Alexander J. McDonald who died after being struck by a snowplow at Boisdale, just eight kilometres south of Barachois Harbour on March 7th. McDonald was a prominent local man, whose accident merited front page – if not entirely accurate – coverage in the Sydney Record of March 9th:

"News reached this city this morning that Alexander J. McDonald, deputy warden of the county, was seriously injured yesterday at Baddeck [sic] by being struck with the I.C.R. snow plough. It appears that while crossing the railway track at Boisedale he became partially embedded in the snow and was unable to move out of the way rapidly enough to avoid the coming snow plough. His lower limbs are said to be badly smashed. Two physicians left North Sydney for the scene of the accident last evening.

LATER.-- It has since transpired that one of Mr. McDonald's feet was so badly crushed that amputation was found necessary. He is still in a critical condition, but the chances are in favour of his recovery."[3]

This last observation proved too optimistic. McDonald died March 21st, never having recovered from his wounds.

His death was not the only railway-related fatality associated with that storm. The Sydney Record of March 15th reported that Michael McMullin of Ball's Creek, near Sydney, died when he was run over by an Intercolonial local train at Sydney River. According to that report, owing to the height of the snow on either side and the fact that McMullin did not see the opening left by the section men for those walking along the track, the unfortunate man was unable to get out of the way in time to escape the approaching train, the driver of which did not see him in time to be able to stop his engine."[4] This death must have seemed especially cruel to islanders. McMullin, 70, was a veteran of the U.S. Civil War. At the time of his death, he was a reviser of the municipal voting lists and a popular local figure. The similarity in the manner of his death and that of McDonald was sure to be the grist of local legend.

The antipathy many Cape Bretoners felt towards the railway often went with them to the grave. An obituary for Stephen MacNeil of Boisdale (who was born in 1825), in the Sydney Post-Record of April 14th 1921, noted:

"He never got reconciled to the new order of things brought about by the railway passing his door. It took everybody by, where as in other days, nearly every wayfarer dropped in and was refreshed."[5]

Above: The *Sydney Flyer* skirts the shores of Lake Bras d'Or in this 1920s era Valentine's postcard. The location is believed to be east of Barrachois. Several "phantom" trains presaged the location of the main line of railway on Cape Breton Island.
(Jay Underwood collection)

Stephen MacNeil was not alone. Fraser's second story has a more pragmatic than supernatural aspect. As she tells it, when the engineers were surveying the Point Tupper to Sydney branch of the Canadian National Railways, they came to a farmhouse and began surveying the land in front of it. The old farmer came out to them and told them that they were wasting their time there; the trains, he said, would pass at the rear of the house, for he had seen them there. The next year a new survey was made, and today the trains pass behind the old farmer's house on what is now the Cape Breton & Central Nova Scotia line.[6]

Railways, while largely popular with residents of urban areas, were often not as well received by rural folk, especially farmers. Few wanted the line to run through their property, dividing the fields, separating barns from yards, and ultimately resulting in a loss of valuable land, often paid for at less-than-market price by government expropriation. The construction of the Intercolonial from Truro to Amherst was littered with cases where farmers sought compensation for damages to their land or increases in the money they received, and the hearings into their claims went on for years after the line opened in 1876.

As a result of such opposition, few preliminary surveys ever marked the "final" route of a railway; the politically-connected farmer could always appeal to his member of either the provincial or federal parliaments and get adjustments made. The Point Tupper-Sydney railway was no exception. After a series of false starts, including one made by American and British capitalists who wanted to build a line to rival that of the Intercolonial, the railway between Port Hawkesbury and Sydney was completed by the Dominion government in 1890 and opened by the Governor General of the day, Lord Stanley of Preston (the same man who created professional hockey's Holy Grail, the Stanley Cup). The line would prove unlucky for one of the men involved with it. The contract engineer, Robert Gillespie Reid – a man of robust health and strength and who went on to found the company that controlled much of the economy of his native Newfoundland for years after his death at age 66 – had his demise brought on by exposure to inclement weather while building the massive railway bridge across Lake Bras d'Or's Barra Strait, between Iona and Grand Narrows.

The third event in Fraser's work was reported from the vicinity of Cape Porcupine, the ominous-looking mountain that overlooks the Strait of Canso (where the railway now crosses the water between the Nova Scotia mainland and Cape Breton island, on a causeway built in 1955) and which blocked the railway's route to Mulgrave, where the trains had previously been put aboard ferries to Port Hastings to continue the trip to Sydney:

"The main highway at Port Hawkesbury, C.B., skirts the cliffs that rise high above the waters of the Strait of Canso, and runs close to the tracks of the C.N.R. Across the narrow ribbon of water, Cape Porcupine casts his dark shadow from the Mulgrave side of the Strait, and busy ferry boats hasten to bridge the mile-wide passage. But time was when the houses on the steep hill above the road looked own on a much less active scene. In these early years, two old women were walking along this highway, when all of a sudden they heard a terrible noise, a rushing and a clatter; then, more terrifying still, an awful, huge, black thing, with one big eye in it, came rattling at them and went right through the fish house that stood near by. They ran to the nearest house, and entered pale, breathless, scared to death. Years later, one of them heard a train on the mainland of Nova Scotia, and recognized the sound as the one she had previously heard. She died before the Inverness railway was built. The track, when surveyed, passed through the fish house. (Fraser added; Told to me by a man who had it first hand.)"[7]

Fraser's reference to Port Hawkesbury and the Inverness railway appears to set this story at about the turn of the last century, as this newspaper report from the Moncton *Transcript* of May 23rd 1901 suggests:

"A Sydney correspondent writes: – "Mckenzie & Mann contracted with R.R. & D.R. McDonald this week to build five miles of railway from Port Hastings to Port Hawkesbury, to connect with the I.C.R. The work, which will give employment to a number of men, will be commenced at once. Sixty men are now employed in extending the wharf at Point Tupper. Engineers are expected at Port Hawkesbury this week with the proposed Southern route from Louisburg to Hawkesbury. It is believed their visit has an important significance."[8]

The significance of the report is that it marks the point when the Inverness and Intercolonial railways met at a nexus with the proposed Cape Breton Railway that eventually went no further than St. Peter's.

These stories are contained in Fraser's chapter on "forerunners," the eerie precursors of usually-fatal events. While Fraser's work – part of what she called an "academic" exercise – lacks the detail one might normally expect in such work, that trains were associated with portents of misfortune is not without some historical fact to support the precept.

While looked upon by the promoters – including Joseph Howe, the province's leading political son and champion of railways – as harbingers of the steady "progress" of society and its economy, railways in the formative years also brought with them death and misery in the form of disease. Among these scourges was typhoid, or typhus, the infectious bacteriological organism found in drinking water, that brought with it symptoms such as a persistent fever ranging from 39° to 40° C. The victim also feels weak, experiencing stomach pains, headache, and loss of appetite, and in some cases may suffer from a rash of flat, rose-colored spots. Although not now fatal if treated in time, a hundred and fifty to two hundred years ago typhoid and cholera would occasionally flare up across the province, associated with infected drinking water. Many of the victims were children and the elderly. These diseases also knew no class distinction; Prince Albert, the consort of Queen Victoria, died of typhoid fever in 1861.

Typhoid did not travel alone; diphtheria was another menace that followed the railway. In her history of Elmsdale, a community in central Nova Scotia, Barbara Grantmyre made note of the tribulations of Reverend John Cameron after the railway had been constructed through the central Nova Scotia village. The line between Truro and Halifax opened officially in December of 1858, but passengers were travelling to Elmsdale by February of that year. Grantmyre notes that ten years after the Rev. Cameron had married and raised a family of five children, diphtheria struck Nova Scotia. In 1858 the disease ravaged at will; the only known remedy was to swab the throat with caustic soda. At Shubenacadie there were 150 cases in this epidemic, with 80 deaths. When the first case appeared in Rev. Cameron's congregation at Elmsdale, he prepared to fight back. He had no caustic soda on hand, so a messenger was sent to the doctor at Shubenacadie asking for the loan of some until a supply could be obtained from Halifax. The messenger came back with a blunt refusal and the threat that Rev. Cameron would be prosecuted if he treated any cases of diphtheria.[9]

Apparently unwilling to use the train connection to Halifax, Rev. Cameron set off for the city on horseback and reached Halifax by noon the next day. There his friend Dr. Parker gave him the necessary medical supplies, and after a short rest the minister started home. Today the journey would take less than two hours; a hundred and fifty years ago, it was a long saddle-sore trip.

"For the next two months he spent day and night among his sick parishioners. His elders told him, 'Forget the sermons, they can wait. Look after the sick.' Now, what he had learned at Philadelphia, the importance of sanitation, the methods of treating the disease, coupled with his own forceful disposition kept the patients alive. John Cameron attended nearly two hundred cases of diphtheria in the district and it is said not one of them died."[10]

Cameron could have shortened his journey by taking the train, but what he had learned at Philadelphia did not extend to understanding how the disease was being spread so rapidly. A long black train could certainly have brought the diphtheria to

Above: Paul Brandon Barringer. This American physician was the first to make the link between unsanitary railway cars and the spread of diseases like typhoid. The ravages of train-borne disease may have led to the notion that death did indeed ride the rails.
(Library of Congress)

Elmsdale. Trains of that era (unlike today when holding tanks are used) were designed to allow toilets to flush directly onto the tracks, except when the train was standing at the station. The realization that trains were responsible for spreading such calamity was slow in coming, but created headlines in the era when railways were just beginning operation in Inverness and Richmond counties. The Halifax *Herald* of December 31st 1903 reported:

"Typhoid Germs Spread in Cars
The roadbed of every railway in America is the deadly zone of fever
New York, Dec. 30 – The roadbed of every railway in America is a deadly zone of typhoid fever infection, a permanent and ever-growing menace to the nation's health.

'The death rate is 56.2 per 100,000 from typhoid fever, while that of England, an old and densely crowded country, is only 18.0. This is due solely to the lack of sanitary appliances in American passenger cars.

Investigation has proved that thousands of cases of typhoid infection are directly traceable to those roadbeds steeped for years in enteric germs blown hither and thither by every wind and every passenger train.'

These startling statements made by Dr. P.B. Barringer, were widely discussed by New York physicians yesterday, and as a result it is quite likely that the legislatures of many states will be asked to compel railways to remove the causes which are responsible for this grave menace to the public health.

In an extended article in the Medical Record Dr. Barringer points out that every mile of railway roadbed in the uncivilized toilet arrangements of the passenger cars, and especially of the Pullman cars [sic].

Every mile of road, he says, is travelled by 85,000 passengers annually. Of this number, he estimates, 375 are typhoid fever patients travelling to their homes during the early stages of infection or during the equally infectious stages of convalescence."[11]

Barringer made the point that contract doctors, working for the corporations that ran the mines and mills, routinely sent sick workers away from the factory once they had been diagnosed, but even the most low-brow hotels and summer resorts turned away suspected typhoid cases. With so many dismissed workers taking the train to find a place in which to convalesce in healthy air, Barringer said it was not surprising that the track itself would become infected, and he blamed "track pollution" that seeped into the rivers and lakes supplying water to communities along the tracks as the cause for the spread of the disease.

Paul Brandon Barringer (1857-1941) was no lightweight. He had earned his medical diplomas at the University of Virginia (1877) and University of the City of New York in 1878. He studied medicine in Europe before returning to the United States to establish the medical preparatory school at Davidson College in North Carolina in 1884. At the time he wrote his article, he was the president of the University of Virginia and would become dean of Virginia Polytechnic Institute.[12]

In short order Pullman cars – which Barringer had labelled "roundly unhealthy" – were being fitted with holding tanks that could be drained at the major terminus after each trip, and the medical community began a renewed battle against typhus, diphtheria, and smallpox that saw the tide turn, and death no longer rode the rails on long black trains as it once had.

NOTES AND REFERENCES

Chapter 1: The Hoodoo Locomotive and the Cobequid Road Ghost

1   Darryl Walsh, *Ghosts of Nova Scotia* (Halifax: Pottersfield Press, 2001), p. 82.
2   Freeman Hubbard, "Superstitions", *Railroad Man's Magazine,* Popular Publications, (April 1949): 44.
3   Moncton *Daily Transcript*, 6 December 1902, p. 1.
4   *Ibid.*
5   This wreck occurred 26 January 1897.
6   Moncton *Daily Transcript*, 6 December 1902, p. 1.
7   Moncton *Daily Transcript*, 8 December 1902, p. 1 *et.seq.*
8   *Ibid.*
9   *Ibid.*
10 http://automatedgenealogy.com/census/cache/index.html
11 Records of the Colchester County Museum.
12 Moncton *Daily Transcript*, 8 December 1902, p. 1 *et.seq.*
13 Halifax *Herald*, 16 December 1902, p. 1.
14 Moncton *Daily Transcript*, 17 December 1902, p. 4.
15 Moncton *Daily Times*, 12 April 1903, p. 1 *et. seq.*
16 Moncton *Daily Transcript*, 3 November 1902, p. 1
17 Halifax *Morning Herald*, 13 April 1903, p. 1
18 *Ibid.*
19 *Ibid.*
20 *Ibid.*
21 *Ibid*
22 *Ibid.*
23 J.F. Gairns, *Railways for All*, 4th edition (London: Ward, Lock & Co., 1923), p. 101.
24 http://www.ble.org/pr/history/page1h.html
25 *Ibid.*
26 *Ibid.*
27 *Ibid.*
28 Halifax *Morning Herald*, 14 April 1903, p. 1.
29 Her name was misspelled "McLowell" in the newspaper reports.
30 http://www.collectionscanada.ca/canadiandirectories
31 http://www.collectionscanada.ca/canadiandirectories
32 http://www.collectionscanada.ca/canadiandirectories
33 Halifax *Chronicle*, 28 February 1890, p. 3.
34 Halifax *Presbyterian Witness*, 8 March 1890, p. 3.
35 *Ghosts of Nova Scotia*, p 82.
36 George R. Stevens, *Canadian National Railways, Volume 1 Sixty Years of Trial and Error* (Toronto: Clarke, Irwin & Co., 1960), p. 217.
37 Moncton *Daily Times*, 16 April 1903, p. 2.
38 Halifax *Herald*, 15 April 1903, p. 1.
39 *Ibid.*

[40] Halifax *Herald,* p. 1.

[41] *Ibid.*

[42] Moncton *Daily Times,* 17 April 1903, p. 2.

[43] *Ibid.*

[44] *Ibid.,* p. 1.

[45] *Ibid.*

[46] *Ibid.*

[47] Halifax *Herald,* 12 May 1903, p. 1.

[48] *Ibid.*

[49] Halifax *Herald,* 18 May 1903, p. 1.

[50] H.B. Jefferson, *The Maritime Express* (Scotian Railway Society, September, 1968), p. 12.

[51] *Ibid.*

[52] *Ibid.*

[53] *Ibid.*

[54] Halifax *Herald,* 3 November 1904, p. 1.

[55] *Ibid.*

[56] New Glasgow *Eastern Chronicle,* 29 December 1902, p. 3.

[57] Moncton *Daily Times,* 4 November 1904, p. 1.

[58] *Ibid.*

[59] Hubbard, p. 44.

[60] http://blues.sk/blues_dictionary.php#25

[61] Isadore H. Coriat, *Abnormal Psychology* (New York: Moffat, Yard and Co., 1921), p. 319

[62] Woodstock *Carleton-Sentinel,* 2 August 1890, p. 1.

[63] Halifax *Chronicle,* 8 June 1900, p. 1.

[64] *Ibid.*

[65] *The Maritime Express,* p. 12.

[66] *Railways for All,* p. 101.

[67] *Railroad Man's Magazine:* 54.

[68] http://www.trainweb.org/j.dimech/roster/460ros1.html

[69] *Railroad Man's Magazine:* 44.

[70] *Ibid.*

[71] *Ibid.*

[72] G.E. McCoy, *Canadian Government Railways Employees Magazine,* (June 1915): 1.

[73] *Canadian Government Railway Employees Magazine,* (December 1914): 75.

[74] W.B. Scott, "Assigned Locomotives", *Canadian Government Railway Employees Magazine,* (July 1915): 18.

[75] *Ibid.*

[76] *Ibid.*

[77] *Ibid.*

[78] *The Maritime Express,* p. 12.

[79] George Drury, *Guide to North American Steam Locomotives* (Waukesha: Kalmbach Books, 1993), p. 232.

[80] Moncton *Transcript,* 14 March 1900, p. 1.

[81] Moncton *Transcript,* 17 March 1900, p. 2.

[82] Moncton *Transcript,* 6 October 1900, p. 2.

[83] *Ibid.*

[84] Quoted by Lance Johnston in *Yonder Comes the Train* (Cranbury: A.S. Barnes & Co., 1965), p. 370.

Chapter 2: *The Harbour Bridge Curse*

[1] Nova Scotia Archives & Records Management Services File "Halifax Bridges" VF116 #1.
[2] *The Skeptic's Dictionary: A Collection of Strange Beliefs, Amusing Deceptions, and Dangerous Delusions* (July 2003), http://skepdic.com/curse.html
[3] *Ibid.*
[4] William James Sidis, *Passaconaway in the White Mountains* (Boston: Richard G. Badger, 1916). See: http://sidis.net/PASSChap7.htm
[5] See http://americanhistory.about.com/od/uspresidents/a/tecumseh.htm
[6] Catherine Martin, http://www.booth.k12.nf.ca/projects/Mi'kmaq/97know9.htm
[7] *Ibid.*
[8] *Ibid.*
[9] *Ibid.*
[10] Halifax *Chronicle-Herald*, 1 April 1985, p. 1.
[11] Chief Dan Paul, private correspondence with the author.
[12] Chief Dan Paul, *We were not the Savages* (Halifax: Fernwood Publishing, 2000), p. 63.
[13] Mrs. William Lawson, *History of the Townships of Dartmouth, Preston and Lawrencetown, Halifax county, N.S.* (Halifax: Morton, 1893), p. 49.
[14] *Ibid.*, p. 19.
[15] *Ibid.*, p. 50.
[16] *Ibid.*, p. 123.
[17] *Ibid.*
[18] Halifax *NovaScotian*, 12 September 1891, p. 3.
[19] Moncton *Daily Times*, 9 September 1891, p. 1
[20] Halifax *Star*, 6 June 1928, p. 3.
[21] Halifax *Herald*, 25 July 1893, p. 2.
[22] *Ibid.*
[23] *Ibid.*
[24] *Ibid.*
[25] *Ibid.*
[26] *Ibid.*
[27] Moncton *Transcript*, 24 July 1893, p. 1.
[28] Moncton *Transcript*, 26 July 1893, p. 2.
[29] Halifax *Acadian Recorder*, Date unknown.
[30] *Scientific American*, 1 October 1898. See: http://www.catskillarchive.com/rrextra/brcorn.Html
[31] Major William Robinson, *Journal of the Nova Scotia House of Assembly 1848 App. 1*, p. 17.
[32] www.trainweb.org/canadianrailways/articles/LegislativeHistoryOfNSRailways.htm
[33] Halifax *Morning Chronicle*, 15 December 1871, p. 3.
[34] *Journal of the Nova Scotia House of Assembly 1848*, p. 15.
[35] Halifax *Morning Chronicle*, 29 December 1867, p. 2.

36 Halifax *Chronicle-Herald*, 1 April 1985, p. 1.
37 Catherine Martin, http://www.booth.k12.nf.ca/projects/Mi'kmaq/97know9.htm
38 Halifax *Chronicle-Herald*, 4 April 1955, p. 1.
39 *Ibid.*
40 *Ibid.*
41 *Ibid.*
42 Nova Scotia Archives & Records Management Service, Halifax Bridge file.
43 *Ibid.*
44 Wilfred Campbell, "Legend of the Restless River", published in *Lake lyrics and other poems* (Saint John: J. & A. McMillan, 1889), p. 60.
45 *Ibid.*
46 http://www.uwo.ca/english/canadianpoetry/confederation/ roberts/criticism/tour_guides.htm

Chapter 3: The White Horse of Merigomish

1   Sigmund Freud, *The Interpretation of Dreams* (1900), p. 87.
2   Halifax *Herald*, 26 January 1901, p. 1.
3   New Glasgow *Eastern Chronicle*, 14 February 1901, p. 1.
4   *Ibid.*
5   New Glasgow *Evening News*, 2 February 1972, p. 3.
6   *Ibid.*
7   *Ibid.*
8   *Ibid.*
9   *Ibid.*
10 *Ibid.*
11 *Ibid.*
12 Tony MacKenzie, "The White Horse Wreck on the Intercolonial", *Canadian Rail*, Canadian Railroad Historical Association, (December 1981): 370.
13 *Revelations 6:8* The *Holy Bible,* King James version.
14 Toronto *Globe*, 27 June 1900, p. 2.
15 Moncton *Daily Transcript*, 15 January 1901, p. 1.
16 *Ibid.*
17 *Ibid.*
18 Fredericton *Daily Gleaner*, 7 September 1901, p. 5.
19 http://www.city.sault-ste-marie.on.ca/library/clergue/francish.htm

Chapter 4: The Grey Lady of Inverness County

1   Robert Frost, *A Boy's Will* (New York: Henry Holt & Co., 1915), p. 12.
2   http://www.bbc.co.uk/wales/northeast/guides/weird/ghosts/pages/greyladies.shtml
3   http://great-castles.com/warkworthghost.html
4   http://www.timetravel-britain.com/05/May/ghosts.shtml
5   http://www.bbc.co.uk/wear/features/2004/04/haunted_house.shtml
6   http://www.castleofspirits.com/glamis2.html
7   http://www.legendsofamerica.com/MO-ColumbiaHauntings.html

[8] William Howitt, *The history of the supernatural in all ages and nations, and in all churches, Christian and pagan: demonstrating a universal faith* (Philadelphia: J.B. Lippincott & Co., 1863), p. 464.

[9] Helen Creighton, *Bluenose Ghosts* (Toronto: Ryerson, 1957), p. 178.

[10] Private interview with the author.

[11] *Ibid.*

[12] Janette MacDonald, *The Historical and Social Development of Judique* (submitted to the Faculty of Arts, St. Francis Xavier University, Antigonish, 1968).

[13] Moses Foster Sweetser, *The Maritime provinces: a handbook for travelers* (Boston: J.R. Osgood, 1875), p. 168.

[14] http://www.trainweb.org/canadianrailways/articles/InvernessRailway.htm

[15] *Ibid.*

[16] Private interview with the author.

[17] Private interview with the author, name withheld by request.

[18] Sydney *Record-Post*, 11 July 1912, p. 1.

[19] John Wilson, private correspondence with the author.

[20] Halifax *Herald*, 12 July 1912, p. 1.

[21] http://www.aaets.org/article55.htm

[22] John Wilson, private correspondence with the author.

[23] *Ibid.*

[24] *Ibid.*

[25] Private interview with author, name withheld by request.

[26] Allistair McBean, *The Inverness and Richmond Railway* (Halifax: Tennant Publishing House, 1987), Table AIII–6.

[27] *Ibid.*

[28] *Ibid.*

[29] *Ibid.*

[30] *Ibid.*

[31] http://groups.msn.com/gypsiewitchcraft/yourwebpage5.msnw

[32] Moncton *Daily Times*, 8 April 1925, p. 8.

[33] Halifax *Morning Chronicle*, 4 April 1925, p. 3.

[34] Halifax *Morning Chronicle*, 7 April 1925, p. 3.

[35] Nova Scotia Archives & Records Management Service, Halifax.

[36] *Ibid.*

[37] *Ibid.*

[38] http://www.seniorwomen.com/articles/articlesNordBreton.html

[39] Private interview with the author.

[40] Mary L. Fraser, *Folklore of Nova Scotia* (Antigonish: Formac Limited, 1975), p. 47.

[41] http://www.prairieghosts.com/maco.html

[42] http://www.virtualsk.com/current_issue/ghost.train,html

Chapter 5: The Whiteside Terror

[1] J. William Calder, *All Aboard* (Antigonish: Formac Limited, 1974), p. 77.

[2] Leona Hussey, Original manuscript, author's collection.

[3] *Ibid.*

4   Leona Hussey, Original manuscript.
5   *Ibid.*
6   http://www.mysteriouspeople.com/Poltergeist-Activity.htm
7   *Ibid.*
8   Private correspondence with the author.
9   Private correspondence with the author.
10 *Ibid.*
11 Antigonish *Casket*, Nova Scotia, 2 February 1905, p. 1.
12 *Ibid.*
13 Walter Hubbell, *The Great Amherst Mystery: A True Narrative of the Supernatural* (Saint John: Daily News Steam Publishing, 1879), p. 10. See also: http://www.gutenberg.org/files/16975/16975.txt
14 http://www.parl.ns.ca/maryellenspook/index.asp
15 http://theshadowlands.net/places/canada.htm
16 *Ibid.*
17 *Ibid.*

Chapter 6: *The Upper Tantallon Ghost*

1   Charles Dickens, "The Signalman", as found in *All The Year Round* (London: Dickens, 1866) and also *Three Ghost Stories* (Whitefish: Kessinger Publishing, 2004), p. 14.
2   The community was originally called French Village, but this name has since been applied to another community further along Route 333.
3   *Halifax Daily News*, 6 June 2005, p. 3.
4   Barbara J. Peart, *As the Last Leaf Fell: From Montbéliard to the Head of St. Margaret's Bay: An illustrated history* (Tantalon: Self-published, 2001), p. 414.
5   Helen Marot, *American Labor Unions* (New York: Henry Holt and Company, 1914). See also: http://www.historyillustrated.com/texts/marot/
6   George Roy Stevens, *Canadian National Railways, Vol. 1: Sixty years of trial and error* (Toronto: Clarke, Irwin & Co., 1960), p. 218. Stevens identifies the community as "Elmdale", but no such place existed along the railway line.
7   http://www.catskillarchive.com/rrextra/chwsagen.Html
8   Bridgewater *Bulletin*, 12 February 1907, p. 1.
9   Bridgewater *Bulletin*, 28 February 1911, p. 1.
10 *Ibid.*
11 *As the Last Leaf Fell*, p. 412.

Chapter 7: *Dealing with the Devil!*

1   Bill Jessome, *More Maritime Mysteries* (Halifax: Nimbus Publishing, 2001), p. 122.
2   *Ibid.*
3   *Folklore of Nova Scotia*, p. 98.
4   http://www.catskillarchive.com/rrextra/chymca.Html
5   Moncton *Daily Transcript*, 2 December 1920, p. 2.
6   Moncton *Daily Times*, 3 December 1920, p. 8.
7   *Canadian National Railways Magazine*, (March 1919): 36.

[8]   Moncton *Daily Times*, 16 February 1925, p. 8.
[9]   New Glasgow *Eastern Chronicle*, 9 March 1923, p. 1.
[10] *Ibid.*
[11] http://www.catskillarchive.com/rrextra/strrmen.Html
[12] Moncton *Daily Times*, 9 May 1929, p. 8.
[13] Amy Pope: "Antigonish", *Catholic World*, Vol. 40, Issue 235 (October 1884): 41-53.

Chapter 8: Roundhouse Ghosts

[1]   http://members.tripod.com/~lindaluelinn/index-43.html
[2]   Bill Jessome, *Maritime Mysteries and the ghosts who surround us* (Halifax: Nimbus, 1999), p. 41.
[3]   http://www.trainweb.org/canadianrailways/articles/SydneyAndLouisburgRailway.htm
[4]   *Ibid.*
[5]   Brian Campbell with A.J.B. Johnson, *Tracks Across the Landscape: The S&L Commemorative History* (Sydney: University College of Cape Breton Press, 1995), p. 16.
[6]   *Maritime Mysteries,* p. 41.
[7]   *Ibid.,* p. 42.
[8]   Antigonish *Casket*, 3 December 1903, p. 1.
[9]   Moncton *The Daily Times*, 15 April 1903, p. 3.
[10] Sydney *Daily Post*, 5 June 1920, p. 1.
[11] Moncton *Daily Times*, 2 February 1920, p. 5.
[12] Sydney *Post Record*, 22 June 1936, p. 3.
[13] Glace Bay *Coastal Courier*, 3 April 1937, p. 1.
[14] *Ibid.*
[15] Sydney *Post Record*, 6 December 1941, p. 1.
[16] *Ibid.*
[18] *Ibid.*
[18] *Maritime Mysteries*
[19] Private correpondence with the author.

Chapter 9: Trains of evil

[1]   *Folklore of Nova Scotia,* p. 45.
[2]   Halifax *Chronicle*, 19 July 1901, p. 1.
[3]   Sydney *Record*, 9 March 1901, p. 1.
[4]   Sydney *Record*, 15 March 1901, p. 1.
[5]   Sydney *Post-Record*, 14 April 1921, p. 2.
[6]   *Folklore of Nova Scotia,* p. 47.
[7]   *Ibid.*
[8]   Moncton *Transcript*, 23 May 1901, p. 1.
[9]   Barbara Grantmyre, "Elmsdale 1785-1914", *Nova Scotia Historical Quarterly*, Vol. 2.2 (1972): 30.
[10] *Ibid.*
[11] Halifax *Herald*, 31 December 1903, p. 3.
[12] http://spec.lib.vt.edu/archives/125th/pres/barring.htm

BIBLIOGRAPHY

In addition to the journals of record quoted in this work, the following sources were also consulted:

Allen, Ralph. *Ordeal by Fire*. New York: Doubleday, 1961.

Beals, Charles Edward Jr. *Passaconaway in the White Mountains*. Boston: Richard G. Badger, 1916.

Calder, J. William. *All Aboard: The history and humour of a "forlorn" little train, and the people and commodities that it carried*. Antigonish: Formac Limited, 1974.

Campbell, Brian. *Tracks Across the Landscape: The S&L Commemorative History*. Louisbourg: Sydney and Louisburg Railway Historical Society, 1995.

Carroll, Robert Todd. *The Skeptic's Dictionary: A Collection of Strange Beliefs, Amusing Deceptions, and Dangerous Delusions*. Indianapolis: John Wiley & Sons, 2003.

Colombo, John Robert. *True Canadian Ghost Stories*. Toronto: Prospero Books, 2003.

Creighton, Helen. *Bluenose Ghosts*. Toronto: McGraw Hill, Ryerson, 1976.

Davenport, Reuben Briggs. *The Death-Blow to Spiritualism*. New York: G. W. Dillingham, 1888.

Drury, George. *Guide to North American Steam Locomotives*. Waukesha: Kalmbach Books, 1993.

Fraser, Mary L. *Folklore of Nova Scotia*. Antigonish: Formac Limited, 1972.

Gairns, J.F. *Railways for All*. London: Ward, Lock & Co., 1920.

Goodspeed Publishing. *Goodspeed's History of Tennessee*. Nashville: The Goodspeed Publishing Co., 1887.

Nova Scotia Historical Quarterly. Journal published quarterly.

Howitt, William. *The history of the supernatural in all ages and nations, and in all churches, Christian and pagan: demonstrating a universal faith*. Philadelphia: J.B. Lippincott & Co., 1863.

Railroad Man's Magazine. Journal published monthly.

Hubbell, Walter. *The Great Amherst Mystery: A True Narrative of the Supernatural*. Saint John: Daily News Steam Publishing, 1879.

Jefferson, H. Bruce. *The Old Hoo-Doo 239*. Halifax: *The Maritime Express*. Scotian Railway Society, September, 1968.

Jessome, Bill. *Maritime Mysteries and the ghosts who surround us*. Halifax: Nimbus, 1999; *More Maritime Mysteries: Everyone has a story*. Halifax: Nimbus, 2001.

Lawson, Mrs. William. *History of the townships of Dartmouth, Preston and Lawrencetown, Halifax county*. Halifax: Morton, 1893.

MacAlpine, David. *MacAlpine's Nova Scotia Directory for 1890-97*. Halifax: MacAlpine Publishing. *MacAlpine's Directory for the City of Halifax 1900-1901*. Halifax: MacAlpine Publishing.

McBean, Allister William Donald. *The Inverness and Richmond Railway*. Halifax: Tennant Publishing House, 1987.

Canadian Government Railway Employees Magazine. Journal published monthly.

MacDonald, Janette. *The Historical and Social Development of Judique*. Antigonish: submitted to the Faculty of Arts, St. Francis Xavier University, 1968.

MacDonald, Laura. *Curse of the Narrows: The Halifax Explosion 1917*. Toronto: Harper Collins, 2005.

MacDougall, J.L. *History of Inverness County*. Strathlorne, 1922.

Canadian Rail. Journal published monthly.

Marot, Helen. *American Labor Unions*. New York: Henry Holt & Company, 1914.

Scientific American. Journal published monthly.

Paul, Daniel. *We were not the Savages*. Halifax: Fernwood Publishing, 2000.

Peart, Barbara J. *As the last leaf fell (From Montbéliard to the Head of St. Margaret's Bay: An illustrated History)*. Tantallon: self-published, 2002.

Catholic World. Journal published monthly.

Roberts, Charles G.D. *The Canadian Guide Book*. New York: D. Appleton, 1891; *The Land of Evangeline and Gateways Thither*. Dominion Atlantic Railway, 1895.

Stevens, George R. *Canadian National Railways, Volume 1 Sixty Years of Trial and Error*. Toronto: Clarke, Irwin & Co., 1960.

Sweetser, Moses Foster. *The Maritime provinces: a handbook for travelers*. Boston: J.R. Osgood, 1875.

Walsh, Darryll. *Ghosts of Nova Scotia*. Halifax: Pottersfield Press, 2000.

INDEX

RMS *Titanic* 69
Robinson, Major William 41, 45
Rocket, locomotive 29
Ruth, George Herman "Babe" 49

S
Sackville, New Brunswick 11
Sackville River, Nova Scotia 37
Sampson, Stephen Patrick 78
Sault Ste. Marie, Ontario 64
Schreiber, Collingwood 105
Scott, W.B. 30
Sidis, William James 35
Slack, Marguerette (Margaret) 12
Slack, Sarah 12
Stanley, Lord, Governor General 108
Starr, John Edward 39
Starr Manufacturing Co. 39
Steele, Stephen; Sydney fatality 101
Stigmatized property 85
St. Peter's, Nova Scotia 77, 108
Sydney & Louisburg Railway (S&L) 97
    wreck at Boisdale 99
    roundhouse fire 100
Sydney Steel Corp. (SYSCO) 28, 58, 98

T
Tecumseh; Curse of 36
Thorpe, Alfred; fatality 16, 27
Toole, Phillip; fatality 10
Tracadie, Nova Scotia 60, 81
Tremaine, Jonathan 38
Trider, Samuel; locomotive engineer 10
    genealogy 12, 30
Triskaidekaphobia 28
Tuft's Cove, Nova Scotia 46
Tupper, Charles; minister of railways 13, 19
Typhoid 109; spread by railway 110

U
Upper Tantallon, Nova Scotia 85, 90

V
Vecsey, George 50
Victoria, Queen 55, 105